Hail to the Chef!

by Russell Kramer

Written by
Tom Connor and Jim Downey

TIME
LIFE
BOOKS

Alexandria, Virginia

MY FELLOW AMERICANS ©1996 Warner Bros.

All recipes ©1996 Time Life Inc. All rights reserved.
TIME-LIFE is a trademark of Time Warner Inc. U.S.A.

No part of this book may be reproduced in any form or by any
electronic or mechanical means, including information storage and
retrieval devices or systems, without prior written permission from
the publisher, except that brief passages may be quoted for reviews.

First Printing. Printed in U.S.A.

Time-Life Custom Publishing

Vice President and Publisher: Terry Newell

Associate Publisher: Teresa Hartnett

Director of New Product Development: Regina Hall

Director of Sales: Neil Levin

Managing Editor: Donia Steele

Project Editor: Sally Collins

Production Manager: Carolyn Mills Bounds

Quality Assurance Manager: James D. King

Design by Laura Campbell

Illustrations by Miles Parnell

All photographs ©1996 Warner Bros.

Books produced by Time-Life Custom Publishing are available
at special bulk discount for corporate and promotional use.
Call 1-800-323-5255.

Connor, Tom.
    Hail to the Chef! / by Russell Kramer:
    Edited and designed by Tom Connor & Jim Downey.
        p.   cm.
    Includes index.
    ISBN 0-7835-4882-6
    1. Cookery, American. 2. Wit and humour, Pictorial. I. Downey,
Jim II. Title.
TX715.C7574   1996
641.5973—dc20   96-33442
                                                                         CIP

TABLE OF CONTENTS

FOREWORD

My fellow former president, Russell Kramer, has written another book. I know this sounds unbelievable, but it's true. The man has been out of office what, five years?, and he's cranked out seven books on his performance as Commander in Chief. And that's just the fiction! It's shameful. Now he's gone and written *Hail to the Chef!: A Taste of Power*. A cookbook! It seems that during his term in office, Kramer cooked for many of his guests, which makes him the only president to leave office with a useful skill. At any rate, despite our rivalry, I've actually tried a few of these recipes. And you know what? They're damn good. They're also damn democratic. I hereby nominate *Hail to the Chef!* as The Official Cookbook of the United States.

Matt Douglas
Former president of the United States
(As portrayed by James Garner)

Shoofly Pie, page 25

NEW ENGLAND & MID-ATLANTIC

New England Clam Chowder

Harvard Beets

Senator Lodge's Bean Soup

Hot German Potato Salad

Red Flannel Hash

Broiled Rib-Eye Steak with Horseradish-Mushroom Cream

Chicken Pot Pie in a Cheese Crust

Waldorf Salad

Yankee Pot Roast

Light Seafood Newburg

Macaroni and Cheddar Bake

Meatball Heroes

Scrod Broiled in Lemon Butter

Rhode Island Jonnycake

Apple Butter

Boston Brown Bread

Maryland Crab Cakes

Shoofly Pie

Autumn Brown Betty

Strawberry Shortcake

Funnel Cakes

Toll-House Cookies

Wellesley Fudge Cake

"*While on a campaign swing through New England, I met a local lobsterman who entertained me for hours with scary tales of the sea and Democrats. His wife was kind enough to sell me this recipe.*"

NEW ENGLAND CLAM CHOWDER

¼ lb. salt pork, diced

1 cup minced onion

3 cups cold water

4 cups diced potatoes

2 dozen shucked hard-shelled clams with their juice, coarsely chopped or 2 (8 oz.) cans chopped clams (about 2 cups)

2 cups heavy whipping cream or light cream

⅛ tsp. thyme leaves

Salt

Freshly ground pepper

2 tbsp. butter, softened

Paprika

Cook and stir the salt pork in a heavy 2-quart saucepan over high heat for about 3 minutes or until a thin film of fat covers the bottom of the saucepan.

Lower the heat to medium and stir in the onion. Cook for about 5 minutes, stirring occasionally, until both the onion and the pork are light golden brown. Add the 3 cups cold water and the potatoes. Bring them to a boil. Lower the heat and simmer, half covered, for about 15 minutes or until the potatoes are just tender.

Stir in the chopped clams, the cream and the thyme and heat just until the boiling point. Season the chowder with salt and pepper and stir in the butter. Serve it in large individual bowls, dusted with a little paprika.

6 to 8 Servings

HARVARD BEETS

12 medium firm young beets

⅓ cup sugar

1½ tsp. cornstarch

½ tsp. salt

⅓ cup red wine vinegar

2 tbsp. butter, cut into ½ inch pieces

Cut the tops off the beets, leaving about 1 inch of the stem. Then scrub them and simmer them, covered, in enough water to cover by 2 inches. Add water during the cooking, if necessary, to keep them covered. This may take from 30 minutes for young beets to 2 hours for older ones.

Drain the beets and reserve ½ cup of the cooking liquid. Then slip off their skins and cut them crosswise into ¼ inch slices. Set them aside.

Mix the sugar, cornstarch, salt and vinegar together in a 2- to 3-quart enameled or stainless steel saucepan. Add the reserved beet cooking liquid and bring it to a boil, stirring constantly, until it's thickened.

Stir in the butter, then stir in the beets; turn the beets to coat them evenly with the sauce. Simmer them for 2 to 3 minutes to heat them through. Adjust the seasoning, put them in a heated bowl and serve at once.

6 to 8 Servings

"Rumors that Lodge used this soup to clear a large area around his table in the Senate Dining Room are completely unfounded. I've been serving it in Washington for years, and I think all that talk is a lot of gas."*

SENATOR LODGE'S BEAN SOUP

4 to 5 qts. water

2 cups (1 lb.) dried pea beans

1 large onion, peeled and pierced with 3 whole cloves

4 sprigs parsley and 1 medium-size bay leaf tied together with kitchen string

2 tsp. plus 1 tbsp. salt

2 (1 lb.) smoked ham hocks

1½ cups minced onion

1 cup minced celery

¼ cup finely chopped fresh parsley

1 tsp. minced fresh garlic

½ tsp. freshly ground pepper

Bring 2 qts. of the water to a boil in a heavy 5- to 6-quart casserole. Add the beans and boil 2 minutes (the water should cover the beans by at least 2 inches; add more water, if necessary). Remove the casserole from the heat and let the beans soak for 1 hour.

Add the onion, the parsley and bay leaf bundle and 2 tsp. of the salt. Bring this to a boil. Lower the heat and then simmer, partially covered, for about 1 hour or until the beans are tender. (Make sure the beans are covered with water during the cooking time.) Throw the onion and parsley and bay leaf bundle away. Then, drain the beans, reserving the cooking liquid. Measure the cooking liquid and add enough water, if necessary, to make 3 quarts.

Return the liquid and the beans to the casserole, then add the ham hocks. Bring this to a boil. Lower the heat and simmer, partially covered, for 2 hours.

Stir in the onions, celery, parsley, garlic, the remaining 1 tbsp. salt and the pepper. Continue to simmer this, partially covered, for 45 minutes.

Remove the ham hocks and throw away the skin and bones. Cut the meat into ½ inch pieces and put them in the soup. Adjust the seasonings and serve it hot.

8 to 10 Servings

HOT GERMAN POTATO SALAD

12 medium red potatoes (about 2 lbs.)

¼ lb. bacon (4 to 6 slices)

1 medium red onion, chopped (about 1¼ cups)

3 tbsp. flour

1½ tbsp. sugar

¾ tsp. salt

¾ tsp. dry mustard

½ tsp. celery seed

½ tsp. pepper

¾ cup water

⅔ cup cider vinegar

3 hard-cooked eggs, coarsely chopped

1 small green pepper, chopped (about ¾ cup)

2 stalks celery, chopped (about 1 cup)

¼ cup chopped parsley

Boil the potatoes in salted water 30 to 35 minutes or until tender; drain. When cool enough to handle, cut them into ¼ inch slices and set them aside.

Meanwhile, in a large nonreactive skillet, cook the bacon until it's crisp. Remove the bacon and reserve the drippings in the skillet.

Cook the onion in the bacon drippings until it's softened, but not browned. Stir in the flour, sugar, salt, mustard, celery seed and pepper. Cook this about 5 minutes on low heat or until the sauce has thickened slightly, stirring constantly.

Stir in the water and vinegar. Then bring this to a boil, stirring constantly, and cook for 1 minute.

Crumble the bacon. Gently stir the bacon and the potato slices into the hot sauce. Cook on medium heat about 1 minute until it is hot and bubbly, stirring gently.

Remove the skillet from the heat and stir in the eggs, green pepper, celery and parsley. Serve the salad warm.

6 to 8 Servings

RED FLANNEL HASH

1 lb. boiling potatoes, peeled and cut into ½ inch cubes

3 small beets, peeled and cut into ½ inch cubes

1¾ cups diced cooked corned beef

1 small onion, chopped

½ cup diced green bell pepper

¼ cup chopped parsley

¼ cup heavy whipping cream

4 tsp. Worcestershire sauce

1 tsp. salt

¼ tsp. pepper

4 to 6 tbsp. butter

Cook the potatoes and the beets separately in boiling water for 10 to 15 minutes or until they're tender. Drain them well.

Mix the potatoes, beets, corned beef, onion, bell pepper, parsley, cream, Worcestershire sauce, salt and pepper together.

In a large skillet, melt 4 tbsp. of the butter over medium-high heat. Add the vegetable mixture and cook and stir it about 10 minutes or until it's golden brown. Add up to 2 more tbsp. butter, if necessary, to keep it from sticking.

Lightly press down on the mixture to form a cake and continue cooking it about 5 minutes or until the bottom has browned.

Take the hash out of the pan and serve it hot.

4 Servings

TIP: To make an even heartier dish, make 4 indentations in the hash with the back of a spoon, break an egg into each indentation, then cover and cook until the eggs are set.

"I've cut some of my best deals in smoke-filled rooms while eating a choice rib-eye steak. The secret is my horseradish sauce. I've seen it bring real tears to Bill Clinton's eyes!"

BROILED RIB-EYE STEAK WITH HORSERADISH-MUSHROOM CREAM

2 boneless rib-eye or club steaks (about 1½ lbs. total)

2 tbsp. butter

1 tbsp. olive or other vegetable oil

4 green onions, coarsely chopped

2 cloves garlic, minced

½ lb. mushrooms, sliced

½ cup beef broth

1 tbsp. cornstarch

2 tbsp. horseradish, drained

1 tsp. thyme leaves

¼ tsp. pepper

¼ cup sour cream

Preheat the broiler. Line a broiler pan with foil.

Put the steaks on the broiler pan and broil them 4 inches from the heat for 7 minutes. Turn them over and broil them for 7 more minutes for rare; 9 minutes for medium-rare; 11 minutes for medium to well done. Let the steaks rest for 5 minutes before slicing them.

In a medium skillet, heat the butter and the oil until the butter is melted. Stir in the green onions and the garlic and cook them about 1 minute or until the onions are translucent. Then add the mushrooms and cook them about 3 minutes or until they're soft.

Mix the beef broth and cornstarch together, then stir them, along with the horseradish, thyme and pepper, into the mixture in the skillet. Bring it to a boil, stirring constantly, and cook for 1 to 2 minutes or until it's slightly thickened. Remove it from the heat and stir in the sour cream.

Serve slices of the steak topped with some of the horseradish-mushroom cream.

4 Servings

CHICKEN POT PIE IN A CHEESE CRUST

Pastry

1½ cups flour

¼ cup grated Parmesan cheese

2 tbsp. minced fresh parsley

½ tsp. salt

¼ tsp. pepper

½ cup cold butter, cut into 8 equal pieces

3 to 4 tbsp. ice water

Filling

2 cups chicken broth

¼ lb. small white onions, peeled and quartered

2 cups peeled and diced yam or sweet potato

¾ to 1 tsp. crumbled sage

¼ tsp. pepper

2 medium carrots, cut into ¼ inch slices

2 cups broccoli florets

½ cup diced celery

¼ cup flour

¼ cup butter, softened

3 cups cooked chicken, cut into bite-size pieces

1 egg, beaten

Make the pastry: Mix the flour, Parmesan cheese, parsley, salt and pepper together. Cut in the butter until the mixture looks like coarse meal. Sprinkle this with 3 tbsp. of the ice water and lightly toss with a fork to form a dough, adding up to 1 more tbsp. water, if necessary, so it can be shaped into a ball. Gather the dough into a ball and divide it in half. Press each half into a disc shape and wrap each in plastic wrap. Refrigerate them for at least 30 minutes.

Make the filling: Bring the chicken broth to a boil in a large saucepan. Then, add the onions, yam, sage and pepper and cook this about 5 minutes or until the yam is just tender. Stir in the carrots, broccoli and celery and cook this about 5 minutes longer or until the carrots are just tender.

In a small bowl, with your fingers, thoroughly blend the flour with the butter. Turn the heat under the vegetable mixture to high, then pinch off pieces of the flour-butter mixture and drop them, one at a time, into the pan, stirring well after each addition.

Cook this 2 to 3 minutes or until the sauce is slightly thickened. Remove the saucepan from the heat, then stir in the chicken.

Preheat the oven to 425°F.

Roll out one disc of the dough on a floured surface into a 12 inch circle and fit it into a 9 inch pie pan. Then spoon the filling into the pie shell.

Roll out the other disc of dough into a 9 inch circle and put it on top of the filling. Trim the extra dough on the bottom and top to within ½ inch of the pie plate. Fold the bottom crust edge over the top crust and crimp it. Cut steam vents in the top and brush it with the beaten egg.

Bake the pie for 15 minutes. Then, lower the oven temperature to 325°F and continue baking for 10 to 15 minutes or until it's golden brown.

Serve the pie hot.

6 to 8 Servings

WALDORF SALAD

3 large firm ripe apples, cut into ½ inch pieces

2 tbsp. fresh lemon juice

3 medium stalks celery, cut into ¼ inch cubes (about 2 cups)

1 cup coarsely chopped walnuts

1 cup mayonnaise

½ cup heavy whipping cream

1 to 2 heads Boston or bibb lettuce, separated into leaves, washed, dried and chilled

Mix the apples, lemon juice, celery and walnuts together in a large bowl.

Mix the mayonnaise and cream together until it's smooth and then pour it over the apple mixture; toss gently, but thoroughly.

Shape the lettuce leaves into 6 or 8 cups on chilled individual serving plates. Divide the salad evenly and spoon it into the lettuce cups. Serve the salads at once.

6 to 8 Servings

YANKEE POT ROAST

½ cup flour

1 tsp. salt

½ tsp. pepper

1 (4 lb.) chuck roast

¼ cup bacon drippings (from frying
about ¼ lb. of bacon)

1 tbsp. vegetable oil

2 cups beef broth

2 cups water

2 cloves garlic, crushed through a press

1 tsp. thyme leaves

1 bay leaf

6 small boiling potatoes, peeled and
quartered (about 1¼ lbs.)

2 to 3 medium white turnips, peeled
and quartered (about 1¼ lbs.)

4 medium carrots, cut into 2 inch pieces

¼ cup chopped parsley

Mix the flour, salt and pepper together. Coat the roast with this mixture, tapping off any excess. Reserve any remaining flour mixture.

Heat the bacon drippings and the oil in a Dutch oven or flameproof casserole over medium heat. Add the roast and brown it slowly, about 30 minutes, turning it to brown all sides. Add more oil, if necessary, to keep it from sticking.

Add the beef broth, water, garlic, thyme and bay leaf. Lower the heat, cover, then simmer for 2 hours, turning the roast occasionally.

Then add the potatoes, turnips and carrots and continue simmering, covered, about 30 minutes, or until the meat and vegetables are tender.

Put the meat and vegetables on a platter and cover them loosely with foil to keep them warm. Throw the bay leaf away.

Slowly, whisk 1 cup of the pot roast liquid into the reserved flour mixture. Put the Dutch oven over medium-high heat and whisk in the flour mixture. Bring it to a boil and cook it 2 to 3 minutes or until it's thickened. Then, stir in the parsley.

Slice the pot roast and serve it with the vegetables and the gravy.

8 Servings

"**M**y wife told me to include this lower-calorie version of what is normally a very rich recipe. Perhaps it could be served with light beer to some lightweight dinner guests. Let's see, what did I do with Douglas's phone number?"

LIGHT SEAFOOD NEWBURG

½ lb. sea scallops

4 green onions

1 cup chicken broth

3 tbsp. sherry, dry white wine or chicken broth

Pinch of cayenne pepper

2 cloves garlic, minced

½ lb. large or medium shrimp, shelled and deveined

3 tbsp. butter

¼ cup flour

½ cup milk

1 can (6 oz.) lump crabmeat, drained

Cut any large scallops in half. Then coarsely chop the green onions, keeping the green and white parts separated.

Combine the chicken broth, sherry, cayenne pepper, garlic and the white part of the green onions in a medium saucepan. Bring it to a boil.

Add the scallops and the shrimp and return the mixture to a boil, stirring constantly. When it begins to boil, remove the scallops, shrimp and the green onion whites and set them aside. Save the broth.

Melt the butter in a large saucepan, then stir in the flour and cook it about 1 minute. Slowly, whisk in the broth mixture until it's smooth. Then blend in the milk.

Return the scallops, shrimp and green onion whites to the sauce. Gently stir in the crabmeat and the green part of the green onions. Cook this about 3 minutes, stirring gently, until the seafood is cooked through.

4 Servings

"**W**hen I was a little boy, I memorized the great speeches of Roosevelt, Churchill and Lincoln, which helped me win my first election: the post of 6th grade blackboard monitor. Lunch in the cafeteria that day was macaroni and cheese. Now, whenever I smell the aroma of this wonderful, heartwarming dish, I think of...Victory!"

MACARONI AND CHEDDAR BAKE

1½ cups uncooked small elbow macaroni (about ½ lb.)

1 cup cottage cheese

1 tbsp. Dijon mustard

⅔ cup sour cream

½ tsp. pepper

2 cups grated sharp cheddar cheese (8 oz.)

1 package (10 oz.) frozen peas

3 tbsp. minced fresh chives or green onions (optional)

Preheat the oven to 400°F. Butter a 1½-quart baking dish.

Cook the macaroni according to the package directions; drain.

Meanwhile, put the cottage cheese and mustard in a food processor and process it until it's smooth. Put this mixture into a large bowl and stir in the sour cream and pepper. Then, stir in the cooked macaroni, 1½ cups of the cheddar cheese, the peas and the chives, if desired. Mix it well.

Put this mixture in the baking dish and sprinkle it with the remaining ½ cup cheddar cheese.

Bake it for about 25 minutes or until it's lightly browned.

6 Servings

MEATBALL HEROES

1 egg white

⅓ cup (packed) parsley sprigs, minced

2 tbsp. tomato paste

2 tbsp. fine plain bread crumbs

3 cloves garlic, minced

1½ tsp. oregano

¾ tsp. salt

½ tsp. pepper

¼ tsp. red pepper flakes

1 lb. ground veal

1 tbsp. olive or other vegetable oil

4 small hero rolls (each about 4½ inches long) or 2 long rolls (each about 9 inches long)

¼ cup mayonnaise

2 tbsp. plain yogurt

½ tsp. lemon juice

2 tsp. grated lemon rind (optional)

2 medium tomatoes, thinly sliced

Preheat the broiler.

In a medium bowl, lightly beat the egg white. Then, beat in 2 tbsp. of the parsley, the tomato paste, bread crumbs, 2 of the garlic cloves, the oregano, salt, pepper and red pepper flakes.

Add the veal to this mixture and mix well. Form it into 24 slightly flattened meatballs, using about 1 heaping tablespoon for each.

In a large nonstick skillet, heat the oil and cook the meatballs about 8 minutes or until they're browned on the outside and well done on the inside. Keep them warm.

Meanwhile, cut the rolls in half lengthwise (for the long rolls, cut them in half crosswise first). Put them on a broiler pan and broil them 4 inches from the heat for 30 seconds to 1 minute or until they're toasted.

Mix the remaining parsley, 1 garlic clove, the mayonnaise, yogurt, lemon juice and lemon rind, if desired, together. For each sandwich, spread a roll with some of the lemon-garlic mayonnaise and top with a few tomato slices and 6 meatballs.

4 Servings

SCROD BROILED IN LEMON BUTTER

6 tbsp. butter, melted

2 tbsp. fresh lemon juice

1 tsp. salt

Freshly ground pepper

2 lbs. skinless fresh scrod (young cod or haddock) fillets

2 tbsp. soft fresh bread crumbs made from homemade-type white bread

Preheat the broiler.

Mix the melted butter, lemon juice, salt and pepper together in a 13 inch x 9 inch baking dish. Then dip the scrod fillets in this mixture to coat them evenly and place them in a single layer in the baking dish.

Broil the scrod 4 inches from the heat for 5 minutes, then baste them with the lemon-butter mixture.

Scatter the bread crumbs over the fish and broil them for 5 minutes more, or until the fish flakes easily with a fork. Serve them at once with the remaining lemon-butter spooned over the scrod.

4 Servings

"This little, insignificant (electoral votes-wise) state is responsible for some of the most...uh, let's see...some events that were crucial to the nation's history, such as...hmm....Well, Rhode Island gave us this recipe!"

RHODE ISLAND JONNYCAKE

1 cup white cornmeal

1 tsp. salt

1 tbsp. butter, softened, plus ¼ cup butter, melted,
   plus 4 butter pats, halved

1 cup boiling water

¼ to ½ cup milk

Maple syrup

Mix the cornmeal, salt and the 1 tbsp. butter together. While stirring constantly, pour in the water in a thin stream. When the butter melts and the water is absorbed, add the ¼ cup milk. Beat this until it holds its shape lightly in the spoon. Stir in up to ¼ cup more milk, a teaspoon at a time, if necessary.

Heat a large griddle or heavy skillet until it's hot. Then brush it with a little melted butter. Ladle ¼ cup of the batter onto the griddle to form each cake, cooking only 1 or 2 at a time and leaving plenty of space between them so they can spread.

Cook the cakes for about 3 minutes on each side or until they're golden brown and crisp around the edges. Keep them warm, loosely covered with foil. If the batter gets too thick, add a little more milk.

Top each cake with half a butter pat and some maple syrup and serve at once.

Eight 5 inch Round Cakes

APPLE BUTTER

5 lbs. tart cooking apples, peeled, quartered and cored

3 cups apple cider

4 cups sugar

Combine the apples and the cider in a 4- to 5-quart enameled or stainless steel saucepan and bring them to a boil. Lower the heat and then simmer, partially covered, for 20 to 25 minutes, or until an apple quarter can be easily mashed with a fork.

Preheat the oven to 300°F.

Purée the apples through the finest blade of a food mill set over a deep bowl, or else rub them through a fine sieve with the back of a spoon. Then stir in the sugar and mix well.

Pour this into a shallow 14 inch x 8 inch baking dish and spread it evenly, smoothing the top with a rubber spatula. Bake it in the middle of the oven for about 2 hours, or until it is thick enough to hold its shape solidly in a spoon. (The traditional test is to put a spoonful of the apple butter on a plate and turn the plate upside down. It should stick to the plate.)

Immediately put the apple butter into hot sterilized pint jars, filling them to within ¼ inch of the top. Seal the jars. Process them in a boiling water bath for 5 minutes.

3 Pints

*"**B**oston is a hotbed of local politics, training ground for the Kennedys and home turf of Tip O'Neil. It's also where I learned to butter my bread on both sides."*

BOSTON BROWN BREAD

1 tbsp. butter, softened	1 cup whole-wheat or graham flour
2 cups buttermilk	1 cup yellow cornmeal
¾ cup dark molasses	1 tsp. salt
¾ cup raisins	¾ tsp. baking soda
1 cup rye flour	

Thoroughly wash and dry two empty 2½ cup (20 oz.) aluminum cans. Then, with a pastry brush, brush the butter over the entire inside surface of each can.

In a deep bowl, beat the buttermilk and molasses together vigorously with a spoon; stir in the raisins. Mix the rye flour, the whole-wheat flour, the cornmeal, salt and soda together. Then, sift them into the buttermilk mixture, 1 cup at a time, stirring well after each addition.

Pour the batter into the cans (it should fill each can to within 1 inch of the top). Cover each can loosely with a circle of buttered wax paper and then with a larger circle of heavy-duty aluminum foil. Shape the foil so it forms a puff like the top of a French chef's hat, allowing an inch of space above the top of the can so the batter can rise. Tie the wax paper and foil in place with kitchen string.

Put the cans on a rack set in a large pot and pour in enough boiling water to come ¾ of the way up the sides of the cans. Bring this to a boil. Lower the heat, cover tightly and steam the bread for 2 hours and 15 minutes.

If you want to serve the bread now, remove the wax paper and foil, turn the bread out of the cans and slice it. If you want to serve it later, leave the bread in the cans with the wax paper and foil left on and reheat them by steaming again for 10 to 15 minutes. The loaves can be kept in the cans in the refrigerator for a week to 10 days.

Two 5½ inch x 3 inch Loaves

MARYLAND CRAB CAKES

1 lb. lump crabmeat

1 cup chopped green onions (about 5 medium)

1 slice firm-textured white bread, torn into large crumbs (about ½ cup)

¼ cup chopped parsley

2 eggs, lightly beaten

2 tbsp. mayonnaise

1 tbsp. Dijon mustard

2 tsp. Worcestershire sauce

¼ tsp. pepper

1 cup fine plain dry bread crumbs

About ¼ cup butter

Hot pepper sauce

Mix the crabmeat, green onions, large bread crumbs, parsley, eggs, mayonnaise, Dijon mustard, Worcestershire sauce and pepper together in a large bowl. Shape this mixture into 12 cakes and roll each cake in the fine dry bread crumbs.

In a large skillet, melt the butter over medium-high heat just until it begins to smoke. Carefully add the crab cakes and cook them in batches, 2 to 3 minutes on each side, or until browned, turning them only once. Add more butter, if necessary, to keep them from sticking.

Serve the crab cakes hot with the hot pepper sauce.

4 Servings

SHOOFLY PIE

Pastry

1½ cups flour

1 tbsp. sugar

¼ tsp. salt

6 tbsp. cold unsalted butter, cut into
    ½ inch pieces

2 tbsp. cold lard, cut into
    ½ inch pieces

3 to 4 tbsp. ice water

Crumb Topping

1 cup flour

½ cup light brown sugar

¼ cup solid vegetable shortening, cut
    into ½ inch pieces

Filling

1 tsp. baking soda

1 cup boiling water

⅔ cup light corn syrup

⅓ cup dark molasses

Sweetened whipped cream or
    vanilla ice cream

Make the pastry: Mix the flour, sugar and the salt together. Add the butter and lard and, with your fingers, rub the ingredients together until it looks like coarse meal. Sprinkle this with 3 tbsp. of the ice water and lightly toss with a fork to form a dough, adding up to 1 tbsp. more water, if necessary, so it can be shaped into a ball. Gather the dough into a ball and dust it with a little flour. Then, wrap it in plastic wrap and refrigerate it for at least 1 hour.

Roll out the dough on a floured surface to a 14 inch circle and fit it into a 9 inch pie pan. Trim the extra dough to within 1 inch of the rim of the pie plate. Fold the extra 1 inch under to make a double thickness and crimp it.

Make the crumb topping: Combine the flour, brown sugar and shortening. With your fingers, rub these together until the mixture resembles coarse meal.

Make the filling: Dissolve the soda in the boiling water, then stir in the corn syrup and the molasses; mix well. Pour this into the unbaked pastry shell and sprinkle it with the crumbs.

Bake the pie for 10 minutes. Then,
lower the oven temperature to 350°F
and continue baking it about 25 minutes
or until the filling is set.

Serve the pie at room temperature with
sweetened whipped cream or vanilla ice
cream.

One 9 inch Pie

"**I** *don't know who this Betty person is, and I don't care. My position on this classic American dessert is that it belongs to all the people. You'll notice I've made few amendments to the recipe, but you don't see me calling it Autumn Brown Russell, do you?*"

AUTUMN BROWN BETTY

⅔ cup apple cider

4 medium apples, peeled and thinly sliced

2 medium pears, peeled and thinly sliced

1 cup golden raisins

⅔ cup dark brown sugar

2 tbsp. lemon juice

1 tsp. cinnamon

½ tsp. ground ginger

1 cup graham-cracker crumbs (8 crackers)

2 tbsp. butter, cut into small pieces

Preheat the oven to 350°F. Lightly butter a 13 inch x 9 inch baking dish.

Bring the apple cider to a boil in a small saucepan. Remove it from the heat, cover it and set it aside.

Toss the apples, pears, raisins, brown sugar, lemon juice, cinnamon and ginger together in a medium bowl until well mixed. Spread half of this mixture in the baking dish, then top it with half of the graham-cracker crumbs. Repeat the layers.

Pour the hot apple cider over the crumb-topped fruit mixture and dot it with the butter.

Bake this for 1 hour and serve it hot or warm.

6 Servings

STRAWBERRY SHORTCAKE

4 cups flour

6 tbsp. sugar plus extra sugar for sprinkling

5 tsp. baking powder

2 tsp. salt

¾ cup cold butter, cut into pieces, plus 6 tsp. butter melted and cooled

1½ cups plus 1 pt. heavy whipping cream

2 pts. fresh strawberries

Preheat the oven to 450°F. Lightly butter a large baking sheet.

Mix the flour, the 6 tbsp. sugar, the baking powder and the salt together in a large bowl. Add the ¾ cup cold butter and, with your fingers, rub the dry ingredients and butter together until it looks like coarse meal. Stir in the cream just until it forms a soft dough. Gather the dough into a ball. Knead it for about 1 minute on a floured surface. Then roll out the dough until it's about 1 inch thick.

With a 3 inch round cutter, cut the dough into 6 rounds. Gather the scraps together, roll out that dough and, using a 2½ inch round cutter, cut it into 6 rounds. Put the 3 inch dough rounds on the baking sheet and brush each with 1 tsp. of the melted butter. Top those with the 2½ inch dough rounds.

Bake them for 12 to 15 minutes or until they're golden brown.

Meanwhile, chop half the strawberries coarsely, leaving the best looking ones for the top. Separate the shortcakes. Put some of the chopped strawberries on the bottom layer, sprinkle them with a little sugar and cover them with the top layer. Garnish the shortcakes with the whole strawberries and serve them with heavy cream.

6 Shortcakes

"**S**ome of my less knowledgeable opponents have described me as sour and bitter. But anyone who really knows me knows I am a big fan of sweets. If you don't believe me, ask my wife. On second thought, just take my word for it."

FUNNEL CAKES

Vegetable oil for deep frying

2 cups flour

1 tbsp. sugar

1 tsp. baking powder

¼ tsp. salt

2 eggs, lightly beaten

1 to 1¼ cups milk

Molasses or maple syrup

Preheat the oven to its lowest temperature. Line 2 large baking sheets with paper towels and put them in the oven. Pour the oil into a large heavy skillet so it's 1½ inches to 2 inches deep and heat it until it's very hot, but not smoking (about 375°F).

Meanwhile, mix the flour, sugar, baking powder and salt together in a deep bowl. Make a well in the center and add the eggs and 1 cup of the milk. Gradually, stir the dry ingredients into the liquid ones until the batter is smooth.

To make the cakes, pour ½ cup of the batter into a funnel that has a tip opening ½ inch in diameter. Keep the tip closed, controlling the flow of the batter with the forefinger of your other hand.

Then, dribble the batter into the hot oil, while moving the funnel in a circle, to make a snail-like coil of 3 or 4 rings about 6 inches in diameter.

Form 1 or 2 cakes and deep-fry them for about 3 minutes on each side, turning them once.

Put the cakes on the baking sheets and keep them warm in the oven. If the batter gets too stiff, add up to ¼ cup more milk, a little at a time.

Serve the funnel cakes warm with molasses or maple syrup.

Twelve 6 inch Cakes

TOLL-HOUSE COOKIES

1 tbsp. plus ½ cup butter, softened

6 tbsp. sugar

6 tbsp. dark brown sugar

½ tsp. salt

½ tsp. vanilla

¼ tsp. cold water

1 egg

½ tsp. baking soda

1 cup flour

1 package (6 oz.) chocolate chips

¾ cup coarsely chopped pecans

Preheat the oven to 375°F. Brush or spread a large baking sheet with the 1 tbsp. butter.

Combine the ½ cup butter, the sugar, dark brown sugar, salt, vanilla and water in a large bowl and beat this with a spoon until the mixture is light and fluffy. Then, beat in the egg and the baking soda. Beat in the flour, ¼ cup at a time. Then, fold in the chocolate chips and pecans.

Using a tablespoon, drop the dough onto the baking sheet 1½ inches apart. With a spatula, gently pat down the tops of each cookie a little bit.

Bake the cookies for about 12 minutes or until they're light brown. Cool them on a rack.

24 Cookies

"**W**hen I was in college, Wellesley girls had a reputation for honesty, integrity, forthrightness and several other virtues. And boy could they bake!*"

WELLESLEY FUDGE CAKE

Cake

4 oz. unsweetened chocolate

1¾ cups milk

½ cup butter, softened

1½ cups sugar

3 eggs

1 tsp. vanilla

1¾ cups cake flour

¼ cup unsweetened cocoa powder

1 tbsp. baking powder

½ tsp. salt

1 cup chopped walnuts

Frosting

4 oz. unsweetened chocolate

¾ cup butter, cut into pieces

½ cup unsweetened cocoa powder

5 cups powdered sugar, sifted

⅓ cup milk

2 tsp. vanilla

1 tsp. lemon juice

Make the cake: Preheat the oven to 350°F. Butter two 8 inch round cake pans, then line the bottoms with circles of wax paper. Butter the wax paper.

In the top of a double boiler, over hot, not simmering, water, melt the chocolate in ½ cup of the milk. Stir this until it's smooth. Let it cool slightly.

In a large bowl, cream the butter and sugar. Beat in the eggs, one at a time, and beat them well after each addition. Then, stir in the chocolate mixture and vanilla and mix well.

Mix the flour, cocoa, baking powder and salt together in a small bowl. Alternate adding the dry ingredients and the remaining 1¼ cups milk to the butter mixture and beat well after each addition. Then, fold in the walnuts.

Spread the batter evenly in the pans and rap the pans once or twice on the counter to remove any air bubbles.

Bake these for 50 minutes, or until a toothpick inserted in the center of the cakes comes out clean.

Cool the cakes in the pans for 5 minutes and then turn them out onto racks to cool completely. Remove the wax paper.

Make the frosting: In the top of a double boiler, over hot, not simmering, water, melt the chocolate. Stir in the butter and cocoa and mix well. Remove it from the heat and gradually beat in, alternating, the powdered sugar and milk, beating well after each addition. Beat in the vanilla and lemon juice.

Frost the cake: Spread a generous amount of frosting over one cake layer. Top it with the second layer, then spread the rest of the frosting over the top and the sides.

One 8 inch Layer Cake

Deep-Dish Peach Pie with Cream-Cheese Crust, page 51

THE SOUTH

Benne Wafers

Virginia Peanut Soup

Red Snapper with Spicy Orange Sauce

Key West Conch Chowder

Louisiana Maque Choux

Shrimp and Chicken Pilau

Shrimp and Ham Jambalaya

Fried Catfish

Sausage Cornbread Stuffing

Honey-Glazed Turkey with Bourbon Gravy

Grillades and Grits

Hush Puppies

Southern Fried Chicken

Southern-Style Black-Eyed Peas

Pollo con Piña a la Antigua

Pasta Jambalaya

Pecan Pie

Deep-Dish Peach Pie with Cream-Cheese Crust

Key Lime Pie

Mint Julep Ice

BENNE WAFERS

1 cup sesame seeds

¼ cup flour

¼ tsp. baking powder

½ cup butter, softened

1 cup light brown sugar

1 egg

1 tsp. vanilla

In a heavy skillet, toast the sesame seeds over low heat for 5 to 7 minutes or until light golden brown, stirring constantly. Set them aside to cool.

Mix the flour and baking powder together in a small bowl.

Cream the butter and sugar together in a medium bowl. Beat in the egg, then the dry ingredients. Stir in the sesame seed and the vanilla.

Put the dough on a sheet of wax paper or plastic wrap and shape it into a log about 1½ inches thick. Then wrap it and refrigerate it overnight or until it's thoroughly chilled.

Preheat the oven to 350°F. Butter a large baking sheet.

Cut the dough into ⅛ inch slices and put them, 3 to 4 inches apart, on the baking sheet.

Bake them for 8 to 10 minutes or until the edges are lightly browned. Cool the wafers for about 30 seconds and then cool completely on a rack.

6 Dozen Wafers

VIRGINIA PEANUT SOUP

2 tbsp. butter

1 medium onion, chopped (about 1¼ cups)

2 cloves garlic, minced

1 cup whole roasted unsalted peanuts plus
    ¼ cup chopped roasted unsalted peanuts

⅔ cup creamy peanut butter

3 cups chicken broth

½ cup light cream or half-and-half

⅛ tsp. ground white pepper

2 tbsp. chopped fresh chives

In a medium skillet, melt the butter. Add the onion and garlic and cook and stir them until the onion is translucent.

Put the butter mixture and the 1 cup whole peanuts in a blender or food processor. Process until it looks like coarse peanut butter. Then, add the creamy peanut butter and process this until it's blended.

With the machine on, gradually add ½ cup of the chicken broth and process it until it's smooth. With the machine still on, add the remaining 2½ cups chicken broth, the cream and the pepper. Process until it's well blended.

Put this mixture in a medium saucepan and simmer it until it's heated through.

Serve the soup hot in individual bowls, sprinkled with the chopped peanuts and the chives.

4 Servings

"**B**elieve it or not, I served in the military with a guy named Red Snapper. He took his poker winnings from the war and opened a little restaurant. Guess what's on the menu?"

RED SNAPPER WITH SPICY ORANGE SAUCE

2 tbsp. flour

¾ tsp. salt

⅜ tsp. pepper

2 red snapper fillets, ¾ inch thick (1 lb. total)

1 tbsp. olive or other vegetable oil

Spicy Orange Sauce

¼ cup butter, softened

1 tbsp. frozen orange juice concentrate

1 tsp. chili powder

2 tbsp. chopped fresh parsley (optional)

Mix the flour, ½ tsp. of the salt and ¼ tsp. of the pepper together in a shallow bowl. Dredge the fish lightly in the flour mixture.

In a large nonstick skillet, heat the oil until it's hot, but not smoking (375°F). Add the fish fillets and cook them about 3 to 4 minutes on each side or until they flake easily with a fork, turning them once.

Meanwhile, make the spicy orange sauce: Mix the butter, orange juice, chili powder, the remaining ¼ tsp. salt and ⅛ tsp. pepper together until it's smooth.

Put the fish on individual dinner plates and top each with 1 tbsp. of the spicy orange sauce. Sprinkle them with parsley, if desired.

4 Servings

KEY WEST CONCH CHOWDER

2 slices bacon, chopped

2 onions, chopped

3 stalks celery, chopped

2 cloves garlic, minced

1 lb. conch meat, minced

1 can (28 oz.) and 1 can (14.5 oz.) unsalted whole tomatoes, coarsely chopped, with their juice

2 cups fish stock or water

1 green bell pepper, minced

1 red bell pepper, minced

1½ tsp. thyme leaves

1½ tsp. oregano

½ tsp. salt

1 tsp. freshly ground pepper

1 bay leaf

2 large boiling potatoes, peeled and cut into ½ inch cubes (about 3 cups)

¼ cup dry sherry (optional)

In a large heavy saucepan, cook the bacon until it's crisp. Remove the bacon and reserve 2 tbsp. of the drippings in the saucepan. Cook and stir the onions, celery and garlic in the bacon drippings about 10 minutes or until the onions are translucent.

Stir in the conch, tomatoes, fish stock, green bell pepper, red bell pepper, thyme, oregano, salt, pepper and bay leaf. Bring this to a boil. Lower the heat, cover and simmer about 2 hours or until the conch is tender. Stir it occasionally to keep it from sticking. If it seems too thick, add a little more fish stock.

Add the potatoes and continue to simmer the chowder about 15 minutes more, or until the potatoes are tender. Remove the bay leaf.

Crumble the bacon. Serve the chowder in individual bowls, sprinkled with some of the bacon. If desired, stir in about 1 tbsp. sherry at the table.

6 Servings

"The *phonetic pronunciation of this recipe is 'Mack-Choo.' You'll know you're saying it right if your dinner guests respond, 'God Bless You.'"*

LOUISIANA MAQUE CHOUX

¼ lb. bacon (4 to 6 slices)

1 large onion, chopped (about 1½ cups)

2 cloves garlic, minced

2 cups fresh or frozen corn kernels

2 medium tomatoes, chopped (about 2 cups)

1 large green bell pepper, chopped (about 1½ cups)

⅓ cup heavy whipping cream

1 tsp. sugar

½ tsp. salt

¼ tsp. cayenne pepper

In a Dutch oven or flameproof casserole, cook the bacon until it's crisp. Remove the bacon and reserve the drippings in the Dutch oven.

Cook the onion and garlic in the bacon drippings about 10 minutes or until the onion is translucent.

Stir in the corn, tomatoes, bell pepper, cream, sugar, salt and cayenne pepper. Bring this to a boil. Lower the heat, then simmer it, partially covered, about 10 minutes or until the corn is tender.

Crumble the bacon and sprinkle it over the corn mixture. Serve it at once.

4 Servings

"Shrimp and Chicken. Some people have said that describes Ross Perot and Bill Clinton. Not me. I didn't say it. Nope, wasn't me."

SHRIMP AND CHICKEN PILAU

6 cups water

1 bay leaf

2½ lbs. chicken, cut up

¼ lb. bacon (4 to 6 slices)

1 cup chopped green onions
(about 5 medium)

1 medium green bell pepper, chopped
(about 1 cup)

2 cloves garlic, minced

1½ cups uncooked rice

1 can (14.5 oz.) whole tomatoes

2 tsp. Worcestershire sauce

1¼ tsp. salt

1 tsp. thyme leaves

½ tsp. pepper

1 lb. medium shrimp, shelled and
deveined

¼ cup chopped parsley

Preheat the oven to 375°F. Butter a 2-quart baking dish.

In a large saucepan, bring the water and bay leaf to a boil. Add the chicken. Then, lower the heat to medium-low, cover and cook it about 30 minutes or until the chicken is tender. Remove the chicken and, when it's cool enough to handle, remove the meat from the bones and cut it into bite-size pieces. Reserve 1¾ cups of the cooking liquid. Throw the bay leaf away.

In a large skillet, cook the bacon until it's crisp. Remove the bacon and reserve the drippings in the skillet.

Cook the green onions, green pepper and garlic in the bacon drippings for 5 minutes. Stir in the rice and cook 5 minutes more, stirring constantly. Then stir in the chicken and put it in the baking dish.

In a large saucepan, bring the reserved cooking liquid, tomatoes, Worcestershire sauce, salt, thyme and pepper to a boil. Pour this over the mixture in the baking dish.

Bake it, covered, for 30 minutes. Then, stir in the shrimp, re-cover it, and bake for 10 minutes. Stir it again, re-cover, and bake 10 more minutes or until the rice is tender and has absorbed all the liquid.

Crumble the bacon. Serve the pilau hot, topped with the parsley and the crumbled bacon.

6 Servings

SHRIMP AND HAM JAMBALAYA

1 cup short-grain white rice, cooked

2 lbs. uncooked medium shrimp, shelled and deveined

6 tbsp. butter

1½ cups minced onion

2 tbsp. minced garlic

1 can (14.5 oz.) whole tomatoes, finely chopped, liquid reserved

3 tbsp. tomato paste

½ cup minced celery

¼ cup minced green bell pepper

1 tbsp. minced fresh Italian parsley

3 whole cloves, ground

1 tsp. salt

½ tsp. thyme leaves

½ tsp. cayenne pepper

¼ tsp. freshly ground pepper

1 lb. cooked lean smoked ham, cut into ½ inch cubes

Cook the shrimp in boiling, salted water for 4 to 6 minutes or until they are pink and firm. Set them aside.

In a heavy 5- to 6-quart casserole, melt the butter. Add the onion and the garlic and cook this until the onion is translucent. Then, stir in the tomatoes with their liquid and the tomato paste and cook for 5 minutes. Stir in the celery, bell pepper, parsley, cloves, salt, thyme, cayenne pepper and pepper and simmer, stirring frequently, until the vegetables are tender and the mixture is thick enough to hold its shape lightly in the spoon.

Add the ham and cook for 5 more minutes, stirring frequently. Then, stir in the shrimp and heat them through. Stir in the cooked rice and cook until the rice has absorbed all the liquid and the mixture is hot.

Adjust the seasoning and serve the jambalaya either from the casserole or from a heated bowl.

6 to 8 Servings

FRIED CATFISH

4 catfish, filleted but not skinned
(about ½ lb. each)
Salt
Freshly ground pepper
Cayenne pepper
1½ cups white cornmeal
2 cups oil for frying

Pat the catfish dry. Then, sprinkle them with salt, pepper and cayenne pepper to taste.

Put the cornmeal on a large flat plate and dredge the catfish in the cornmeal, shaking off any extra cornmeal. Let the catfish sit a few minutes so the cornmeal will stick.

Fill a heavy 12-inch skillet with about ½ inch of the oil and heat it just until it begins to smoke. Then, add the catfish and cook them about 5 minutes on each side or until they're golden brown and flake easily with a fork. Drain them on paper towels and serve them hot.

4 Servings

*"**I**f there's one single dish that symbolizes the South to me, it's cornbread. Unless you count Phyllis George, but she's not single."*

SAUSAGE CORNBREAD STUFFING

Cornbread

1½ cups flour

½ cup yellow cornmeal

⅓ cup dark brown sugar

2½ tsp. baking powder

1 cup buttermilk or 1 cup milk mixed
  with 1 tbsp. vinegar or lemon juice

6 tbsp. butter, melted

1 egg, lightly beaten

Stuffing

½ lb. spicy bulk sausage, crumbled

2 tbsp. butter

1 cup chopped leeks or onion

2 stalks celery, chopped (about 1 cup)

1 clove garlic, minced

1 small red bell pepper, chopped
  (about 1 cup)

¼ cup chopped parsley

1 tsp. crumbled sage

1 tsp. thyme leaves

1 tsp. salt

½ tsp. pepper

Preheat the oven to 425°F. Butter an 8 inch square baking dish.

Make the cornbread: Mix the flour, cornmeal, brown sugar and baking powder together in a deep bowl and make a well in the center. Stir the buttermilk, melted butter and egg together. Pour the liquid ingredients into the dry ingredients and, gradually, stir them together just until blended. Do not mix too much.

Spread the batter evenly in the pan and bake it for 25 to 30 minutes or until a toothpick inserted in the center comes out clean. Cool the cornbread in the pan on a rack for 10 minutes and then turn it out onto a rack and cool it completely.

Preheat the oven to 250°F. Cut the cornbread into ¾ inch cubes and put them in a single layer on a baking sheet. Bake them about 1 hour or until they're dry and crisp.

Make the stuffing: Cook the sausage in a large skillet over medium heat for 5 to 10 minutes or until it's no longer pink inside. Stir in the butter, leeks, celery and garlic and cook them about 5 minutes or until the leeks are softened. Then, increase the heat to medium-high, add the bell pepper and cook it for 3 minutes.

Stir in the dried cornbread cubes, the parsley, sage, thyme, salt and pepper. Cool it slightly before using.

10 Cups Stuffing

HONEY-GLAZED TURKEY WITH BOURBON GRAVY

1 (12 lb.) turkey

Sausage Cornbread Stuffing
  (the recipe precedes)

1 tbsp. salt

1 tsp. pepper

½ cup honey

1 tbsp. soy sauce

2 cups bourbon

1 tbsp. butter

3 tbsp. flour

Preheat the oven to 350°F.

Stuff the turkey loosely with the Sausage Cornbread Stuffing and truss it. Rub the outside of the turkey with the salt and the pepper. Then, put the turkey, breast-side-up, in a roasting pan.

Mix the honey and soy sauce together, then drizzle it over the turkey to coat it completely. Pour the bourbon into the bottom of the roasting pan and cover the pan tightly.

Bake the turkey for 2½ hours, keeping it covered. Then, baste the turkey with the pan juices and roast it, uncovered, for 20 to 30 minutes or until the internal temperature of the thickest part of the leg is 170°F, basting the turkey once or twice. Cover the parts that are browning too quickly with foil.

Let the turkey rest for 15 minutes before carving.

Meanwhile, pour the pan juices into a bowl (there should be about 3 cups). Melt the butter in a small saucepan and stir in the flour, and then ¼ cup of the pan juices. Cook this until the mixture is smooth and brown. Gradually, whisk in the remaining pan juices and cook it until it's thickened.

Spoon the stuffing into a serving dish, carve the turkey and serve it with the gravy.

12 Servings

“**I've always loved grits for breakfast, and I heard Huey Long loved them for hors d'oeuvres, lunch and midday snacks. Here's a great way to have them for dinner.**”

GRILLADES AND GRITS

¼ lb. bacon (4 to 6 slices)

4 boneless veal round steaks, ½ inch thick (about ¼ lb. each)

⅓ cup flour

1½ tsp. salt

¼ tsp. pepper

1 medium red onion, chopped (about 1⅔ cups)

1 small yellow or green bell pepper, chopped (about ⅔ cup)

1 stalk celery, chopped (about ½ cup)

2 cloves garlic, minced

1 can (14 oz.) whole tomatoes

2 tbsp. tomato paste

2 tsp. Worcestershire sauce

2 tsp. red wine vinegar

½ tsp. basil

¼ tsp. red pepper flakes

1 bay leaf

5 cups water

1 cup hominy grits

In a large skillet, cook the bacon until it's crisp. Remove the bacon and reserve the drippings in the skillet.

Pat the veal steaks dry. Mix the flour, ½ tsp. of the salt and the pepper together in a shallow bowl. Then dredge the veal in the flour mixture, shaking off any extra.

Heat the bacon drippings until they're hot, but not smoking (375°F). Add the veal steaks and cook them 2 to 3 minutes on each side until they're browned. Remove the veal steaks.

Add the onion, bell pepper, celery and garlic to the skillet and cook and stir them about 10 minutes or until they're softened. Then, stir in the tomatoes, tomato paste, Worcestershire sauce, red wine vinegar, basil, red pepper flakes, the bay leaf and ½ tsp. of the salt.

Add the veal steaks and bring the mixture to a boil. Lower the heat and simmer, partially covered, about 1 hour or until the veal steaks are tender, turning them occasionally. Discard the bay leaf.

Meanwhile, about 30 minutes before the veal steaks are done, bring the water and the remaining ½ tsp. salt to a boil in a medium saucepan. Stirring constantly, slowly pour in the grits, make sure the water keeps boiling. Lower the heat, cover and simmer this for 15 to 20 minutes, stirring occasionally. Remove the grits from the heat and let them stand, covered, for a few minutes.

Crumble the bacon. On individual dinner plates, put the veal steaks on top of some of the grits and top them with the pan juices and crumbled bacon.

4 Servings

"**A** *lot of men and women ease the stress of political life with the demon alcohol, but not me. When I come home after a hard day of agreeing with people, nothing calms me down faster than a plate of hush puppies.*"

HUSH PUPPIES

2 to 3 cups vegetable oil for deep frying

1 cup sifted flour

1 cup yellow cornmeal

4 tsp. baking powder

½ tsp. salt

1 egg, lightly beaten

⅔ cup buttermilk

⅓ cup minced onion

Heat the oil in a Dutch oven or heavy skillet until it's hot, but not smoking (375°F).

Mix the flour, cornmeal, baking powder and salt together in a large bowl. Add the egg, buttermilk and onion and stir it until it's well blended.

Drop the batter by rounded teaspoonfuls into the hot oil and cook them about 3 to 5 minutes, or until they're golden brown, turning them frequently.

Serve the hush puppies hot.

About 32 Hush Puppies

"**H**ave you ever woken up in the morning and felt like your blood was a bit thin? Or maybe that you needed a little meat on your bones because that exercise program has you looking like one of those scrawny marathon runners? This recipe will fix the damage done by any austerity program."

SOUTHERN FRIED CHICKEN

1 (2 to 2½ lb.) chicken, cut into serving pieces
½ cup flour
1½ tsp. salt
½ tsp. freshly ground pepper
⅓ cup buttermilk
⅓ cup lard
5 tbsp. butter
Lemon wedges and watercress (**optional**)

Pat the chicken dry. Mix the flour, salt and pepper together in a paper or plastic bag. Dip the chicken in the buttermilk and then put 1 or 2 pieces at a time in the bag and shake it to coat the chicken with the flour mixture.

In a large heavy skillet, melt the lard and the butter over high heat and heat it until it's hot, but not smoking (375°F). Add the chicken thighs and legs and cook them about 3 minutes on each side, or until they're lightly browned. Add the chicken breasts and cook on one side for 3 minutes. Then, turn all the chicken and add the wings.

Continue cooking and turning until all of the chicken pieces are evenly browned, a total of 20 to 30 minutes. Drain the chicken between double thicknesses of paper towels.

Put the chicken on a platter and garnish it with lemon wedges and watercress, if desired.

4 Servings

SOUTHERN-STYLE BLACK-EYED PEAS

1 lb. shelled fresh black-eyed peas

⅓ cup water

1 tbsp. salt

1 slice bacon, or 2 pieces lean salt pork, each about 2 inches square

1½ tbsp. fresh savory or 1½ tsp. dried savory

3 tbsp. butter

2 tbsp. chopped fresh parsley

Put the peas, water, salt, bacon, savory and 2 tbsp. of the butter in a medium-size saucepan. Bring this to a boil. Lower the heat, then simmer it, uncovered, for 12 to 15 minutes, or until the peas are tender and most of the liquid has evaporated.

Remove the bacon and gently stir in the parsley and the remaining 1 tbsp. butter. Serve the peas at once.

6 Servings

" **A**s most people are aware, what Matt Douglas knows about cuisine could fit in a teaspoon. Case in point: He tasted the subtle nuance of rum in this chicken dish and from that moment on called it Chicken Piña Colada. Classy."

POLLO CON PIÑA A LA ANTIGUA

1 (3½ to 4 lb.) chicken, cut into
  6 serving pieces

¼ cup fresh lime juice

1½ tsp. salt

Freshly ground pepper

¼ cup olive oil

1 cup minced onion

1 tsp. minced garlic

3 medium tomatoes, peeled, seeded and
  minced or 1 cup minced and drained
  canned tomatoes

¼ cup raisins

1 tbsp. grated lime rind

½ tsp. oregano

2 cups minced fresh pineapple

¼ cup medium-dark rum

Pat the chicken dry. Then rub each piece with the lime juice and sprinkle with the salt and pepper. Let the chicken sit for 5 minutes or so.

Heat the oil in a large heavy skillet until it's hot. Add the chicken, 2 or 3 pieces at a time, and cook them until they're evenly browned. Put the chicken on a plate.

Add the onion and garlic to the skillet and cook and stir them about 5 minutes or until the onion is translucent. Return the chicken to the skillet. Lower the heat, cover the skillet tightly, and simmer this for 30 minutes.

Add the tomatoes, raisins, lime rind and oregano and turn the chicken pieces to coat them evenly with the mixture. Cover the skillet again and simmer it for 10 more minutes or until the chicken is tender and the juices run clear.

Meanwhile, cook the pineapple in a small saucepan over high heat, stirring frequently, until it is reduced to 1 cup.

In another small saucepan, heat the rum over low heat. Off the heat, ignite the rum and slide the pan gently back and forth over the range until the flame dies. Stir the rum into the pineapple.

Add the pineapple-rum mixture to the chicken and simmer it about 3 minutes or until it's heated through. Adjust the seasonings.

Put the chicken on a heated platter and pour the pineapple-rum mixture over it.

6 Servings

PASTA JAMBALAYA

1 tsp. olive or other vegetable oil

¼ lb. bulk spicy sausage or spicy sausage links, casings removed

1 large onion, coarsely chopped

3 cloves garlic, minced

1 large green bell pepper, coarsely chopped

1 stalk celery, coarsely chopped

1 can (14.5 oz.) whole tomatoes

½ tsp. salt

¼ tsp. hot pepper sauce

Pinch of cayenne pepper

1 bay leaf

¾ lb. fusilli pasta or other medium pasta shape

½ lb. skinless boneless chicken breasts, cut into ¼ inch strips

In a large skillet, cook the sausage in hot oil for 2 to 3 minutes or until it's no longer pink inside. Add the onion and garlic and cook and stir this about 5 minutes or until the onion begins to brown.

Stir in the bell pepper, celery, tomatoes, salt, hot pepper sauce, cayenne pepper and the bay leaf. Bring it to a boil. Lower the heat, cover and simmer while you cook the fusilli.

Cook the fusilli according to the package directions; drain and keep it warm.

Add the chicken to the sausage mixture and cook it about 5 minutes or until it's tender and no longer pink, stirring frequently. Remove the bay leaf.

Serve the sausage mixture over the fusilli.

4 Servings

"One *piece of this rich dessert will satisfy your sweet tooth. Two pieces will satisfy Bill Clinton's. Three, and your dentist will be sending you Christmas gifts."*

PECAN PIE

Pastry	*Filling*
1¼ cups flour	4 eggs
⅛ tsp. salt	2 cups dark corn syrup
4 tbsp. cold vegetable shortening or lard	2 tbsp. butter, melted
2 tbsp. cold butter, cut into ¼ inch pieces	1 tsp. vanilla
	1½ cups pecans
3 tbsp. ice water	

Make the pastry: Mix the flour and the salt together. Add the shortening and the butter and, with your fingers, rub the ingredients together until the mixture looks like coarse meal. Sprinkle this with the ice water and lightly toss with a fork to form a dough. Gather the dough into a ball and dust it with a little flour. Then, wrap it in plastic wrap and refrigerate it for at least 30 minutes.

Preheat the oven to 400°F.

Lightly butter a 9 inch pie pan. Roll out the dough on a floured surface to a 14 inch circle and fit it into the pie pan. Trim the extra dough to within ½ inch of the rim of the pie plate. Fold the extra ½ inch under to make a double thickness and then crimp it.

To keep the unfilled pie shell from shrinking as it bakes, either set another pie plate that has been lightly buttered on the underside into the pie shell or line it with a sheet of lightly buttered foil.

Bake the pie shell for 8 minutes. Remove the pan or foil and let the pie shell cool while you make the filling.

Make the filling: Beat the eggs for about 30 seconds. Then, slowly pour in the corn syrup and continue beating until it is well blended. Beat in the melted butter and the vanilla, then stir in the pecans.

Carefully pour the filling into the pie shell. Then, bake it for 35 to 40 minutes or until the filling is firm.

Serve the pie warm or at room temperature.

One 9 inch Pie

DEEP-DISH PEACH PIE WITH CREAM-CHEESE CRUST

Pastry

½ cup butter, softened

½ package (8 oz. package) cream cheese, softened

1¼ cups flour

2 tbsp. sugar

¼ tsp. salt

2 tbsp. heavy whipping cream

Filling

1½ lbs. fresh peaches, peeled and thinly sliced (8 to 10 medium)

2 tbsp. brown sugar

1 tbsp. flour

3 tbsp. butter, melted

2 tsp. vanilla

1 egg yolk, lightly beaten with 2 tsp. cold water

1 tsp. sugar

Make the pastry: Beat the butter and cream cheese together with a spoon until it's smooth and fluffy. Mix the flour, sugar and salt together and add it to the butter mixture. Then, add the cream and, with your hands or a spoon, mix it until it forms a dough. Gather the dough into a ball and dust it with a little flour. Then, wrap it in plastic wrap and refrigerate it while you make the filling.

Preheat the oven to 350°F.

Make the filling: Gently mix the peaches, brown sugar, flour, melted butter and vanilla together. Spread this mixture evenly in an 8 inch x 8 inch x 2½ inch baking dish.

Roll out the dough on a floured surface to a 10 inch or 11 inch square. Carefully, put it on top of the filling. Crimp the edges of the dough so it sticks to the dish. Brush the dough with the egg yolk-water mixture, then sprinkle it with the sugar. Cut 2 small slits in the top.

Bake the pie for 35 to 40 minutes or until it's golden brown.

One 9 inch Pie

"I *once gave a speech in the Florida Keys to the largest group of people I've ever seen sleeping in one place at one time. It must have been the hot weather."*

KEY LIME PIE

Crust
11 graham crackers
⅓ cup butter, melted
2 tbsp. sugar

Filling
3 whole eggs plus 3 egg yolks
1 can (14 oz.) sweetened condensed milk
⅔ cup fresh lime juice (about 6 limes)
1 tbsp. grated lime rind
Unsweetened whipped cream

Preheat the oven to 375°F.

Make the crust: Put the graham crackers in a food processor or blender and process them until they become fine crumbs. Mix them with the melted butter and sugar. Then, press them evenly into a 9 inch pie pan to form a crust.

Bake it for 8 to 10 minutes or until the crust just begins to brown. Cool the crust while you make the filling.

Lower the oven temperature to 350°F.

Make the filling: Whisk the whole eggs and egg yolks together, then whisk in the sweetened condensed milk. Stir in the lime juice and the grated lime rind.

Carefully, pour the filling into the crust and bake it for 10 to 12 minutes or until it's just set. Let the pie cool for 1 hour, then refrigerate it for 4 to 6 hours or until it's chilled.

Serve the pie with unsweetened whipped cream.

One 9 inch Pie

*"**I** got this recipe in the Blue Grass State, home of the Kentucky Derby. I think, like a good horse, this dessert should have a kick!"*

MINT JULEP ICE

3 cups water

1¼ cups sugar

1 cup (loosely packed) fresh mint plus
    2 tbsp. chopped fresh mint

¾ cup bourbon

Juice of 2 lemons

8 mint sprigs

Mix the water, sugar and the 1 cup mint together in a heavy saucepan. Bring this to a boil over medium heat, stirring to dissolve the sugar. When the mixture reaches a boil, cover the pan and boil it for 1 minute. Then, pour the mixture through a fine sieve into a medium bowl and allow it to cool to room temperature. Refrigerate it for about 30 minutes or until it's cold.

Mix the 2 tbsp. chopped mint, the bourbon and the lemon juice together. Stir this into the chilled sugar mixture and freeze it until it's firm, using one of the methods below.

To serve, scoop ½ cup of the mint julep ice into each of 8 sherbet dishes or mint julep cups. Garnish each with a mint sprig.

8 Servings

Freezing Methods

Hand Method: Put the mixture into a nonreactive metal bowl and put it in the freezer. When it starts to get firm around the edge, either whisk it or beat it with an electric mixer to break up the ice crystals. Repeat this process until it is frozen through. Then freeze 15 more minutes after the last whisking or beating.

Food Processor Method: Put the mixture into a nonreactive metal bowl and put it in the freezer. When it has become hard, with the center still a little soft, break it up into chunks and put them in the food processor. Process them until the mixture is smooth, but not melted. Return the mixture to the bowl and freeze 15 more minutes.

Churning Method: Freeze the mixture using an electric ice cream maker. Follow the manufacturer's instructions.

Meat-and-Potatoes Loaf, page 59

THE MIDWEST

Herbed Wild Rice

Honey-Glazed Pork Tenderloin

Schnitz und Kneppe

Meat-and-Potatoes Loaf

Cheese-Topped Vegetable Hash

Herbed Parmesan Oven Fries

Tart Red and Green Coleslaw

Veal Stroganoff

Noodles with Lamb and Carrots

Corn Custard

Chocolate Pudding Cake

Honey-Graham Crackers

Sliced Watermelon Sorbet

Peanut Butter Cup Pie

Chocolate-Chip Devil's Food Cake

"You probably associate wild rice with the lakes of Northern Minnesota, but Washington knows a thing or two about it, too. Take Gary Hart. He had some pretty wild Rice when he was a Senator."

HERBED WILD RICE

2 tbsp. butter

¼ cup chopped onion

1 cup uncooked wild rice

1 tbsp. chopped fresh parsley

1 tbsp. chopped fresh chives or 1 tsp. freeze-dried chives

1 tbsp. chopped fresh thyme or 1 tsp. dried thyme

½ tsp. salt

Freshly ground pepper

2½ cups water

In a medium-size saucepan, cook the onion in the butter about 2 minutes or until it's soft. Stir in the wild rice until it is coated with the butter. Then, stir in the parsley, chives, thyme, salt, pepper and water. Bring this to a boil. Lower the heat, cover and then simmer for 30 to 35 minutes or until all the liquid has been absorbed and the wild rice is tender, but still a little crunchy.

4 to 6 Servings

HONEY-GLAZED PORK TENDERLOIN

3 green onions

1 quarter-size slice (¼ inch thick) fresh ginger, unpeeled

2 cloves garlic

¼ cup frozen apple juice concentrate

2 tbsp. reduced-sodium regular soy sauce

2 tbsp. honey

¼ tsp. pepper

1½ lbs. lean center-cut pork tenderloin

Preheat the broiler or get the grill ready. If broiling, line a broiler pan with foil.

Mince the green onions, ginger and garlic in a food processor. Scrape into a bowl and add the apple juice concentrate, soy sauce, honey and pepper. Brush the pork with some of this mixture.

Broil the pork on the foil-lined broiler pan or grill 4 inches from the heat 30 to 40 minutes or until golden brown. Every 7 minutes or so, turn the pork and brush with the glaze. Then cut the pork into thin slices to serve.

6 Servings

"Isn't 'Schnitz und Kneppe' the phrase JFK uttered during his historic visit to Berlin? Well, it's a memorable dish anyway."

SCHNITZ UND KNEPPE

2 cups dried apples (½ lb.)	*Dumplings*
3 lbs. smoked ham butt	2 cups flour
6 cups chicken broth	1 tbsp. baking powder
2 tbsp. dark brown sugar	¼ tsp. salt
	2 tbsp. butter, cut into ¼ inch pieces and softened
	1½ cups milk

Soak the apples in water at room temperature at least 8 hours or overnight; drain.

Place the smoked ham butt in a heavy 5- to 6-quart casserole at least 12 inches in diameter. Pour in enough water to cover the ham by at least 2 inches. Bring to a boil, then simmer, partially covered, for 1½ hours or until the ham is pierced easily and deeply with the point of a small skewer or a sharp knife. Put the ham on a plate and throw the cooking liquid away.

Cut the ham into ¼ inch cubes. Return the ham to the casserole and add the apples, chicken broth and brown sugar.

Bring this to a boil, stirring until the sugar dissolves. Lower the heat, then simmer, partially covered, for 15 minutes. Taste for seasoning.

Prepare the dumplings: Combine the flour, baking powder and salt in a deep bowl. Add the butter and, with your fingers, rub the flour and butter together until it looks like coarse meal. Add the milk and beat this vigorously with a spoon until smooth.

Drop this by heaping tablespoonfuls on top of the simmering ham mixture. Cover the casserole tightly and simmer, undisturbed, for 10 minutes or until the dumplings are puffed and fluffy and a toothpick inserted in the center of one comes out clean.

Remove the dumplings and pour the ham mixture into a bowl or deep platter; top with the dumplings.

6 Servings

*"**D**ouglas and I met Elvis in the men's room on the train while eluding Tanner and his minions. Later, in the dining car, I overheard The King order four portions of this meat-and-potatoes loaf. So you know it's gotta be good."*

MEAT-AND-POTATOES LOAF

5 medium carrots, cut into 1 inch pieces

1 large yellow or red bell pepper, cut into large pieces

½ lb. lean ground beef

½ lb. ground veal

5 medium green onions, minced

⅔ cup bottled barbecue sauce

¾ cup fine plain bread crumbs

2 tbsp. tomato paste

3 tbsp. butter, melted

1 tbsp. brown sugar

1 tsp. basil

1 tsp. pepper

¾ tsp. salt

1¼ lbs. red potatoes, unpeeled

1 tbsp. flour

1 egg

⅓ cup grated Parmesan cheese

Preheat the oven to 425°F. Butter a shallow 2-quart casserole.

Boil the carrots and the bell pepper just until the carrots are tender, about 7 minutes. Drain.

Mix the beef, veal, green onions, barbecue sauce and ½ cup of the bread crumbs.

Put the carrots, bell pepper, tomato paste, 1 tbsp. of the melted butter, brown sugar, the remaining ¼ cup bread crumbs, basil, ¼ tsp. of the pepper and ½ tsp. of the salt in a food processor. Process just until mixed.

Shred the potatoes using the food processor. Toss with the flour.

Beat together the egg, remaining 2 tbsp. melted butter, ¾ tsp. pepper and ¼ tsp. salt. Mix with the potatoes.

Spread half the potatoes in the bottom of the casserole. Spread with the carrot-pepper mixture, then the meat mixture, then the remaining potatoes. Sprinkle with the Parmesan cheese.

Bake this about 1 hour or until the meat is cooked through and the top is golden brown.

6 Servings

"Clinton always said he didn't inhale. Horse hockey! It wouldn't hurt his standing in the polls if he inhaled some of my veggie hash."

CHEESE-TOPPED VEGETABLE HASH

1 lb. all-purpose potatoes, cut into ½ inch cubes

1 lb. butternut or acorn squash, peeled and
    cut into ½ inch cubes

1 tbsp. olive oil

½ lb. mushrooms, quartered

2 green bell peppers, diced

1 large onion, chopped

1 clove garlic, minced

½ cup evaporated skim milk

½ tsp. salt

½ tsp. thyme leaves

¼ tsp. freshly ground pepper

⅓ cup shredded cheddar cheese

Cook the potatoes and squash in boiling water about 10 minutes or until they are tender; drain.

Meanwhile, in a large ovenproof skillet, cook and stir the mushrooms, bell peppers, onion and garlic in the oil about 8 minutes or until the bell peppers are tender.

Preheat the broiler.

Add the potatoes and squash, evaporated milk, salt, thyme and pepper to the skillet. Bring this to a boil. Lower the heat, cover, then simmer about 5 minutes to blend the flavors. Remove the cover and cook about 3 minutes or until the liquid is absorbed.

Sprinkle the hash with the cheddar cheese and broil it 4 inches from the heat for 2 to 3 minutes or until the cheese is melted.

4 Servings

HERBED PARMESAN OVEN FRIES

1½ lbs. baking potatoes, peeled

⅓ cup grated Parmesan cheese

½ tsp. oregano leaves

¼ tsp. rosemary

¼ tsp. freshly ground pepper

¼ tsp. salt

Preheat the oven to 400°F. Cut the potatoes lengthwise into ¼ inch slices, then cut them again lengthwise into ¼ inch sticks. Put them in a large bowl and lightly spray them with nonstick cooking spray; toss them to coat with the spray.

Add the Parmesan cheese, oregano, rosemary and pepper; toss again.

Put the potatoes on 2 baking sheets and spread them out in a single layer so they can brown evenly. Bake them for about 40 minutes, turning them over every 10 minutes, or until they are golden brown and crisp.

Pile the fries on a platter, sprinkle them with the salt and serve.

4 Servings

"**F**ormer President Douglas gripes about me publishing a cookbook: 'Did William Howard Taft write Thirty Days To A Slimmer Ass?,' he asks. The answer is no, but Taft might have lived longer had he eaten fewer desserts and more of my slaw."

TART RED AND GREEN COLESLAW

6 cups shredded red cabbage (about ½ lb.)

6 cups shredded green cabbage (about ½ lb.)

1 small red bell pepper, slivered (about 1 cup)

½ cup sour cream

½ cup plain yogurt

⅓ cup mayonnaise

2 tbsp. cider vinegar

1 tsp. caraway seed

1 tsp. mustard seed

1 tsp. salt

¼ tsp. pepper

Toss the cabbages and red bell pepper together in a large serving bowl. Mix the sour cream, yogurt, mayonnaise, vinegar, caraway seed, mustard seed, salt and pepper and pour over the vegetables; toss them to combine. Put the coleslaw in the refrigerator until it's chilled.

6 to 8 Servings

VEAL STROGANOFF

¼ cup domestic dried mushrooms

¼ cup paprika

1 tsp. salt

2 to 3 tsp. freshly ground pepper

2 lbs. lean veal (from leg round roast), cut into 2 inch x ½ inch x ¼ inch strips

¾ cup butter

1 medium onion, minced

2 cloves garlic, minced

1 (6 oz.) can tomato paste

½ cup vodka

½ lb. uncooked spinach noodles

½ lb. uncooked plain egg noodles

¼ cup plus 2 tbsp. chopped parsley

2 tbsp. poppy seed

1 cup sour cream

1 tbsp. lemon juice

Soak the mushrooms in boiling water for 15 to 20 minutes. Drain; save 2 cups of the soaking liquid. Then, strain that liquid and set it aside. Mince the mushrooms.

Mix the paprika, salt and pepper together on wax paper, then dredge the veal strips in this mixture.

Heat ½ cup of the butter in a Dutch oven until it turns golden brown. Brown the veal in the butter in small batches. Remove all the veal from the Dutch oven.

Add the onion, garlic and mushrooms to the Dutch oven and cook and stir them for 7 minutes. Stir in the reserved soaking liquid, the tomato paste and the vodka and bring this to a boil. Lower the heat, add the veal and cook this for 10 to 15 minutes.

Meanwhile, cook the noodles separately according to the package directions; drain. Melt the remaining ¼ cup butter. Toss each kind of noodle with 2 tbsp. of the melted butter, 2 tbsp. of the chopped parsley and 1 tbsp. of the poppy seed; keep them warm.

Mix the sour cream and the lemon juice together. Remove the veal mixture from the heat and gently stir in the sour cream mixture. Do not reheat it.

Pile the veal mixture in the center of a large platter and surround it with the spinach and the egg noodles. Sprinkle with the remaining parsley.

8 Servings

NOODLES WITH LAMB AND CARROTS

2 tbsp. cornstarch

¾ lb. lean boneless lamb (from the leg), cut into 2 inch x ¼ inch strips

2 tbsp. olive or other vegetable oil

3 cloves garlic, minced

4 green onions, cut into 1½ inch pieces

3 medium carrots, thinly sliced

¾ cup beef broth

2 tbsp. lime juice

1 tsp. honey

2 tbsp. chopped fresh mint or 2 tsp. dried mint

1 tsp. grated lime rind (optional)

¼ tsp. pepper

¾ lb. uncooked thin egg noodles

1 cup frozen peas

Place the cornstarch in a plastic bag. Add the lamb strips and toss them to coat.

In a large skillet, cook the garlic and the green onions in 1 tbsp. oil for about 3 minutes or just until the garlic begins to brown. Add the remaining 1 tbsp. oil and the lamb, then cook and stir about 6 minutes or until the lamb is browned. Remove the lamb mixture from the skillet and set aside.

Combine the carrots, beef broth, lime juice, honey, mint, grated lime rind, if desired, and pepper in the skillet. Bring this to a boil. Lower the heat, cover, and simmer while the noodles are cooking.

Cook the noodles according to the package directions. Three minutes before the noodles are done, uncover the carrot mixture and bring it to a boil again. Add the lamb mixture and the peas. Heat this through, about 3 minutes.

Drain the pasta and top it with the lamb mixture. Serve it right away.

4 Servings

My wife Margaret, a great first mate, and a very knowledgeable food critic.

RUSSELL KRAMER FOR PRESIDENT COMMITTEE

The sweet taste of victory. The honeymoon lasted exactly four years.
Then came the divorce.

*There's going to be a picture of me dancing with a giant dog
in every newspaper on the planet tomorrow.*

I hold one truth to be self evident—that simple deeds, like writing a great American cookbook, are the stepping stones to immortality.

I agree that my only handicap was that I couldn't control Congress.
But with my natural swing, I've never gotten stuck in a bad lie.

Sometimes it's important to get back to the basics.
Here I'm helping Douglas with the concept that
the little white ball is supposed to go in the hole.

I believe that there are times to take a stand.
But sometimes the smartest thing to do is
get the heck out of town. With dignity, of course.

I always put my faith in the good judgement of the American people.
O.K., everybody makes a mistake sometimes.

Haney always had the gift for gab. When his political career comes to a close, I think he might want to consider car sales.

Even the "King of Rock and Roll" occasionally hears the call of nature.

You'd be scared, too, if a man in ruby slippers with a trumpet approached you on the street.

I've always loved traveling the back roads of this great country.
It gives me a chance to meet folks up close and personal.

President Haney. Proof that, under our democratic system, just about anyone can become president.

There are two things in life better than winning an election.
One of them is Rita's Cream Puffs.

You know, there are good days and bad days.
But on my worst day, I would never sit on top of the desk
of the President of the United States.

Matt and I on the campaign trail.
Nothing keeps you young like smiling 24 hours a day.

*"**I** believe Gen. George Custer improvised this tasty dessert in the field shortly before he won the Battle of Little Big Horn. He lost? Good, I never could stomach glory-seeking warmongers!"*

CORN CUSTARD

2 cups fresh corn kernels, cut from about 4 large ears of corn,
  or 2 cups frozen corn, completely thawed

4 eggs

1 cup heavy whipping cream

½ cup milk

¼ cup flour

1 tbsp. sugar

1 tsp. salt

⅛ tsp. ground white pepper

Preheat the oven to 350°F. Put the corn in a blender and blend at high speed for 30 seconds. Scrape the sides, then blend until it's puréed. Add the eggs, cream, milk, flour, sugar, salt and pepper and blend again until it's smooth and thick.

Pour this mixture into a 1½-quart soufflé dish and put the dish in a deep roasting pan set on the middle shelf of the oven. Pour in enough boiling water to come about ⅔ of the way up the sides of the dish.

Bake this for about 1 hour or until golden brown and a knife inserted in the center comes out clean. Serve at once.

4 to 6 Servings

"**W**hite House kitchen records reveal massive amounts of my chocolate pudding cake missing from the pantry on June 21, July 10 and again on August 3. Funny, but those are precisely the dates Rush Limbaugh visited 1600 Pennsylvania Avenue!"

CHOCOLATE PUDDING CAKE

1 cup cake flour

½ cup plus ⅓ cup sugar

6 tbsp. unsweetened cocoa powder

2 tsp. baking powder

¼ tsp. salt

½ cup low-fat milk

2 tbsp. safflower oil

1½ tsp. vanilla

¼ cup chopped walnuts

⅓ cup light brown sugar

1 cup water

1 tbsp. powdered sugar

Lightly butter a 9 inch pie pan and dust it with some unsweetened cocoa powder.

Sift the cake flour, ½ cup of the sugar, 3 tbsp. of the cocoa powder, the baking powder and the salt into a large bowl. Add the milk, oil and 1 tsp. of the vanilla and stir it to combine. Then stir in the walnuts and spread the batter evenly in the pie pan.

Mix the remaining ⅓ cup of the sugar, the remaining 3 tbsp. cocoa powder and the brown sugar together. Then stir in the remaining ½ tsp. vanilla and the 1 cup water. Pour this carefully over the batter in the pie pan.

Microwave this at 50% for 18 to 20 minutes, turning the dish a quarter turn every 3 minutes.

Sift the powdered sugar over the cake and serve it warm.

10 Servings

HONEY-GRAHAM CRACKERS

⅓ cup butter, softened

¼ cup light brown sugar

1 egg

1 tbsp. milk

1 tsp. baking soda

¼ cup honey

1½ to 2 cups whole-wheat flour

1 cup flour

½ tsp. salt

Preheat the oven to 375°F.

Beat the butter, brown sugar and the egg together in a medium bowl until smooth and creamy.

Stir the milk and baking soda together, then add them to the butter mixture. Stir in the honey.

Add 1½ cups of the whole-wheat flour, the flour and the salt and stir this until it forms a dough. You can add up to ½ cup more whole-wheat flour if the dough is too sticky. Shape the dough into a ball and divide it into four portions.

Liberally dust a baking sheet with whole-wheat flour. Put one portion of the dough in the center of it and roll it out to a little larger than a 9 inch x 4½ inch rectangle. Using a ruler, trim the rectangle to that exact size. With a knife, lightly mark the dough into eight 2¼ inch squares, being careful not to cut all the way through. With a fork, prick each square. Or you can mark it with a small cookie cutter, being careful not to cut it all the way through.

Bake the dough for 10 to 12 minutes or until golden brown. Cool for 2 to 3 minutes on the baking sheet and then carefully separate into individual crackers and put them on a rack to cool completely. Shape and bake the rest of the dough.

32 Crackers

TIP: Whole-grain flours, like whole-wheat, don't keep as well as more refined or processed flours, like all-purpose, so keep them in the refrigerator or freezer.

"**W**hat mother wouldn't be proud of a son who could whip up a batch of cool watermelon sorbet on a hot summer day? It's just one of the many recipes I received when I marched in the Gay Pride Day parade."

SLICED WATERMELON SORBET

1 watermelon (about 8 lbs.)
1 cup superfine sugar
2½ tbsp. fresh lemon juice
1 cup fresh blueberries

Cut the watermelon in half lengthwise, then scoop out all the flesh and put it into a large bowl. Pick the best looking watermelon half for serving and throw away the other half.

Cut the watermelon shell crosswise into 1 inch thick slices and then put the slices back together so it looks like the original shell. Freeze this until it's rock-hard and the slices are stuck together. It helps to prop the shell in place, so the slices remain together.

Meanwhile, purée the watermelon flesh in several batches using a blender or food processor. Then press this purée through a sieve to get rid of the seeds. You should have about 6 cups of strained fruit. If you have more or less, add or subtract the amount of sugar accordingly by 2 tbsp. for each 1 cup of fruit.

Stir the sugar and lemon juice into the strained fruit and then freeze it using one of the following methods. Whichever method you use, do not stir the blueberries into the watermelon sorbet until the end of its freezing period.

Fill the frozen watermelon shell with the sorbet. Smooth the top so it looks like a freshly cut watermelon half. Then freeze it until it is completely solid—at least 2 hours.

When you're ready to serve it, present the watermelon complete and then, using the pre-cut lines as a guide, cut the watermelon into slices.

12 to 16 Servings

Freezing Methods

Hand Method: Put the mixture into a nonreactive metal bowl and put it in the freezer. When it starts to get firm around the edge, either whisk it or beat it with an electric mixer to break up the ice crystals. Repeat this process until it is frozen through. Then freeze 15 more minutes after the last whisking or beating.

Food Processor Method: Put the mixture into a nonreactive metal bowl and put it in the freezer. When it has become hard, with the center still a little soft, break it up into chunks and put them in the food processor. Process them until the mixture is smooth, but not melted. Return the mixture to the bowl and then freeze 15 more minutes.

Churning Method: Freeze the mixture using an electric ice cream maker. Follow the manufacturer's instructions.

"*I could just see Jimmy Carter whipping up a pie like this in the White House kitchen. Too bad he didn't get a second term to try it, either.*"

PEANUT BUTTER CUP PIE

Gingersnap Crust

35 (2 inch) gingersnaps (about 9 oz.)

½ cup butter, melted

2 tbsp. sugar

Filling

3 oz. semisweet chocolate

1 tbsp. butter

1½ cups creamy or chunky peanut butter

⅓ cup brown sugar

1 cup milk

½ cup light cream or half-and-half

1 tsp. vanilla

Make the crust: Put the gingersnaps in a food processor or blender and process them until they become fine crumbs. Mix them with the melted butter and sugar. Then press them evenly into a 9 inch pie pan to form a crust.

Make the filling: Melt the chocolate and the butter in a small heavy saucepan over low heat, stirring until it's smooth. Set it aside to cool.

Beat the peanut butter until it's softened, then gradually beat in the brown sugar. Add the milk, the cream and the vanilla and continue beating until it's smooth.

Pour the peanut butter mixture into the crust and then pour in the melted chocolate mixture. Gently swirl them together, but do not blend them completely.

Cover the pie with plastic wrap and freeze it for at least 6 hours or overnight. Before serving, let it stand at room temperature for 15 minutes.

One 9 inch Pie

CHOCOLATE-CHIP DEVIL'S FOOD CAKE

Cake

4 oz. unsweetened chocolate, cut into large pieces

1 cup milk

2¼ cups flour

1 tsp. baking powder

¼ tsp. salt

½ cup butter, softened

1⅓ cups dark brown sugar

3 eggs

1 tsp. vanilla

1½ cups chocolate chips

Frosting

¾ cup sugar

½ cup light brown sugar

1 cup heavy whipping cream

4 oz. unsweetened chocolate, cut into large pieces

½ cup butter, cut into pieces

Make the cake: Preheat the oven to 350°F. Butter two 8 inch round cake pans, then line the bottoms with circles of wax paper. Butter the wax paper, then flour the pans.

In the top of a double boiler, over hot, not simmering, water, melt the chocolate in ¼ cup of the milk. Stir this until it's smooth. Let it cool slightly.

Mix the flour, baking powder and salt together in a small bowl. Set this aside.

In a large bowl, cream the butter and the dark brown sugar. Beat in the eggs, one at a time, and beat them well after each addition. Then beat in the vanilla. Beat in the chocolate mixture and the remaining ¾ cup milk. Then beat in the dry ingredients and stir in the chocolate chips.

Spread the batter evenly in the pans and rap the pans once or twice on the counter to remove any air bubbles.

Bake these for 30 to 35 minutes, or until a toothpick inserted in the center of the cakes comes out clean.

Cool the cakes in the pans for 10 minutes and then turn them out onto racks to cool completely. Remove the wax paper.

Make the frosting: Bring the sugar, the light brown sugar and the cream to a boil in a small, heavy saucepan, stirring constantly. Lower the heat and simmer for 6 minutes without stirring.

Remove the pan from the heat and stir in the chocolate and butter until both are melted. Beat this mixture 12 to 15 minutes or until it is cooled, thick and creamy.

Frost the cake: Spread a generous amount of frosting over one cake layer. Top it with the second layer, then spread the rest of the frosting over the top and the sides.

One 8 inch Layer Cake

Tex-Mex Barbecued Chicken with Salsa, page 81

THE SOUTHWEST

All-American Corn Pasta with Chilies and Tomato

Black Bean Salad with Smoked Mozzarella

Layered Turkey Enchilada Casserole

Bowl of Red

Sloppy Josés

Pasta with Chicken in Jalapeño Tomato Sauce

Fajitas with Stir-Fried Chicken

Tex-Mex Barbecued Chicken with Salsa

Grilled Beef and Fresh Salsa in Flour Tortillas

Mariachi Vegetables (Calabacitas)

Tex-Mex Lattice-Topped Pie

Mexican Rice

Red, Gold and Green Skillet Casserole

Posole

Sopaipillas

Fresh Fruit Salad with Mint and Coconut

"**T**hey're saying I took a kickback while in office. Hah! They want a kick-back? Let 'em eat my corn pasta with chilies!"

ALL-AMERICAN CORN PASTA WITH CHILIES AND TOMATO

Pasta Dough

¾ cup finely ground cornmeal

¾ cup bread flour

1 egg

1 egg white

3 tbsp. water

1 tbsp. virgin olive oil

Sauce

1 tbsp. safflower oil

5 cloves garlic, peeled and thinly sliced

2 small diced red chilies, finely chopped or ½ tsp. red pepper flakes

1 green bell pepper, chopped

1¾ tsp. salt

1 large tomato, peeled, seeded and minced

1 tbsp. red wine vinegar

1 tbsp. unsalted butter

Make the pasta dough: Mix the cornmeal and flour together in a large bowl. Whisk the egg, egg white and water together in a small bowl. Make a well in the center of the dry ingredients and pour in the egg mixture. Gradually stir the dry ingredients into the liquid ones and when almost all the dry ingredients are moistened, add the olive oil and work it into a dough by hand.

On a lightly floured surface, knead the dough. If the dough is stiff and crumbly, knead in a little water, a teaspoon at a time, and, if the dough is too sticky, knead in a little flour, a tablespoon at a time, until the dough pulls away from the work surface and it's soft and pliable—10 to 15 minutes. Then, wrap it in plastic wrap and let it rest for 15 minutes.

Dust the work surface with some cornmeal and roll out the dough into a 2 foot x 9 inch rectangle. Cut the rectangle into ½ inch wide strips and set them aside. Bring 3 quarts of water to a boil.

Prepare the sauce: In a large skillet, cook and stir the garlic and chilies in the oil until the garlic is light brown. Add the bell pepper and ¼ tsp. of the salt and cook and stir this for 5 minutes. Then, stir in the tomato, vinegar and butter and cook for 2 more minutes.

Add the remaining 1½ tsp. salt to the boiling water. Add the dough strips and cover the pan. When the water returns to a boil, uncover it and cook the pasta for 6 minutes. Drain well and add it to the sauce in the skillet. Toss to combine.

4 Servings

BLACK BEAN SALAD WITH SMOKED MOZZARELLA

4 (6 inch) corn tortillas, each cut into 6 wedges

⅓ cup reduced-sodium chicken broth or
    reduced-sodium vegetable broth

3 tbsp. fresh lemon juice

1 tbsp. tomato paste

¾ tsp. tarragon

½ tsp. salt

¼ tsp. hot pepper sauce

2 cans (16 oz.) black beans, rinsed and
    drained

6 green onions, thinly sliced

1½ cups cherry tomatoes

⅓ cup chopped parsley

3 oz. smoked mozzarella, diced

1 large onion, diced

3 cloves garlic, minced

⅓ cup water

1 oz. Canadian bacon, diced

Preheat the oven to 400°F. Put the tortilla wedges on a baking sheet and bake them for 5 minutes or until they're lightly crisp. Set them aside.

Meanwhile, whisk the chicken broth, lemon juice, tomato paste, tarragon, salt and hot pepper sauce together in a large bowl. Add the black beans, green onions, tomatoes, parsley and mozzarella and toss them to combine.

In a large skillet, cook the onion, garlic, water and bacon about 5 minutes or until the onion is softened and the liquid has evaporated. Add this to the black bean mixture and toss it to combine.

Spoon the black bean salad onto a serving platter and surround it with the tortilla wedges.

4 Servings

"I *knew a lot of turkeys when I was in Washington. I had to get through twenty layers of them to get a bill passed."*

LAYERED TURKEY ENCHILADA CASSEROLE

1 can (16 oz.) tomato sauce

1 can (4 oz.) diced green chilies

1 clove garlic, minced

1 tbsp. chili powder

2 tsp. ground cumin

1 tsp. oregano

¼ tsp. pepper

9 corn tortillas

½ lb. cooked turkey, cut into 2 inch x ¼ inch x ¼ inch strips

6 to 8 green onions, coarsely chopped

1 package (10 oz.) frozen corn kernels, thawed

2½ cups grated cheddar cheese (about ¾ lb.)

Preheat the oven to 375°F. Lightly butter a shallow 1-quart baking dish.

Mix the tomato sauce, chilies, garlic, chili powder, cumin, oregano and pepper together.

Put 3 of the corn tortillas, overlapping them, on the bottom of the baking dish. Spread them with ⅓ of the tomato mixture.

Then, cover the tomato mixture with half of the turkey, green onions and corn. Sprinkle with 1 cup of the cheddar cheese. Top the cheese with 3 more tortillas, half of the remaining tomato mixture, all of the remaining turkey, green onions and corn and 1 cup of the cheese.

Top the cheese with the remaining 3 tortillas, the remaining tomato mixture and the remaining ½ cup cheese.

Bake it, uncovered, for 25 minutes and serve the casserole hot.

6 Servings

BOWL OF RED

¼ cup vegetable oil

1 medium red onion, chopped
(about 1½ cups)

3 cloves garlic, minced

2½ lbs. beef chuck, cut into ½ inch cubes

⅓ cup chili powder

1 tbsp. ground cumin

2 tsp. oregano

1 tsp. paprika

1 can (28 oz.) crushed tomatoes

2 cups beef broth

1 tsp. salt

⅓ cup yellow cornmeal

¼ cup water

2 cans (15 oz. each) pinto beans, rinsed and drained

1 cup chopped green onions (about 5 medium)

In a Dutch oven or flameproof casserole, cook the onion and garlic in the oil over medium heat about 10 minutes or until the onion is translucent.

Increase the heat to medium-high, add the beef and cook and stir it about 10 minutes or until it's lightly browned.

Stir in the chili powder, cumin, oregano and paprika, then stir in the tomatoes, beef broth and salt. Bring this to a boil. Lower the heat, cover and simmer it about 1½ hours or until the beef is tender.

Fifteen minutes before serving, mix the cornmeal and water together. Bring the beef mixture back to a boil and stir in the cornmeal mixture and pinto beans. Lower the heat, cover and then simmer it about 5 minutes or until the beans are heated through and the sauce is thickened, stirring occasionally.

Sprinkle the chili with the green onions and serve it hot.

8 Servings

"**M**att Douglas traded his $1,500 suit jacket for a compass and this recipe from Ernesto back there in the ditch after we jumped from the train. By the taste of it, I'd say Matt got the better deal."

SLOPPY JOSÉS

2 tsp. vegetable oil

1 medium onion, coarsely chopped

1 small green bell pepper, coarsely chopped

3 cloves garlic, minced

1 lb. lean ground beef

⅔ cup chili sauce

1 tbsp. tomato paste

2 to 3 drops hot pepper sauce

1 tbsp. chili powder

1 tbsp. ground cumin

¼ tsp. salt

¼ tsp. pepper

4 hamburger buns, toasted

In a large skillet, cook and stir the onion, bell pepper and garlic in the oil until the onion begins to brown.

Add the beef and cook and stir it about 5 minutes or until it's no longer pink. Then, stir in the chili sauce, tomato paste, hot pepper sauce, chili powder, cumin, salt and pepper. Bring this to a boil. Lower the heat, cover and simmer it for 15 minutes.

Spoon the hot beef mixture onto the buns.

4 Servings

PASTA WITH CHICKEN IN JALAPEÑO TOMATO SAUCE

2 tbsp. olive or other vegetable oil

1 medium onion, coarsely chopped

3 cloves garlic, minced

2 skinless boneless chicken breast halves, cut into bite-size pieces (about ½ lb. total)

1 tbsp. butter

1 tbsp. ground cumin

1½ tsp. oregano

1 tbsp. flour

1 can (28 oz.) crushed tomatoes

1 tbsp. tomato paste

2 small pickled jalapeño peppers, seeded and minced

1 package (10 oz.) frozen corn kernels

¼ tsp. salt

¼ tsp. pepper

¾ lb. uncooked small pasta shells (about 3½ cups)

¼ cup (packed) cilantro sprigs, coarsely chopped (optional)

In a large skillet, cook and stir the onion and garlic in 1 tbsp. of the oil just until the onion begins to brown. Add the remaining 1 tbsp. oil and the chicken and cook and stir this about 5 minutes or until the chicken is browned. Put the chicken mixture in a bowl, loosely covered, and set it aside.

Then, add the butter to the skillet and heat it until it's melted. Add the cumin and oregano and cook and stir them for 30 seconds. Stir in the flour and cook about 30 more seconds.

Stir in the tomatoes, the tomato paste, the jalapeño peppers, the corn, salt and pepper and bring this to a boil. Lower the heat, cover and simmer it while you cook the pasta.

Cook the pasta according to the package directions; drain and keep it warm.

Stir the reserved chicken mixture and the cilantro, if desired, into the tomato sauce. Serve the chicken mixture over the pasta.

6 Servings

FAJITAS WITH STIR-FRIED CHICKEN

½ cup lemon juice

6 tbsp. chopped fresh cilantro or parsley (optional)

4 tsp. ground cumin

2 tsp. cornstarch

1 tsp. salt

½ tsp. pepper

1 lb. skinless boneless chicken breasts, cut into ¼ inch strips

1 cup mild red or green salsa

2 tbsp. vegetable oil

8 flour tortillas, warmed

8 large romaine lettuce leaves, shredded

½ cup sour cream

Mix 6 tbsp. of the lemon juice, 2 tbsp. of the cilantro, if desired, the cumin, cornstarch, salt and pepper together in a small bowl. Stir in the chicken and set it aside.

Mix the salsa and the remaining 2 tbsp. lemon juice and 4 tbsp. cilantro, if desired, together in another small bowl and set it aside.

In a medium skillet, add the vegetable oil. Cook and stir the chicken over medium-high heat about 5 minutes or until it's tender and no longer pink.

To serve, put the tortillas, shredded lettuce, the salsa mixture and the sour cream in serving dishes. Diners make their own fajitas by topping a tortilla with some of each of the ingredients, ending with a little sour cream, and then rolling it up.

4 Servings

TIP: The tortillas can be warmed either in a 200°F oven for 5 to 10 minutes, wrapped in foil, or in the microwave at 100% for 1 minute, wrapped in a damp paper towel.

TEX-MEX BARBECUED CHICKEN WITH SALSA

1½ cups mild salsa

2 tsp. chili powder

1 tsp. honey

1 tsp. ground coriander

¾ tsp. ground cumin

4 skinless boneless chicken breast halves
  (about 1 lb. total)

½ cup frozen corn kernels, blanched

1 tbsp. fresh lime juice

Preheat the broiler or get the grill ready. If broiling, line a broiler pan with foil.

Mix the salsa, chili powder, honey, coriander and cumin together in a medium bowl. Put 1 cup of this mixture and the chicken in a shallow dish, turning the chicken to coat it with the mixture. Refrigerate it for 20 minutes.

Stir the corn and lime juice into the salsa mixture in the bowl.

Put the chicken on the foil-lined broiler pan or grill. Broil or grill it 6 inches from the heat for about 8 minutes or until the chicken is tender and the juices run clear.

Put one chicken breast on each of 4 dinner plates and top them with the salsa-corn mixture.

4 Servings

GRILLED BEEF AND FRESH SALSA IN FLOUR TORTILLAS

2 tbsp. fresh lime juice

2 tbsp. tequila or gin

1½ tsp. chili powder

½ tsp. oregano

¼ tsp. ground cumin

Freshly ground pepper

1 lb. bottom round steak, cut into ½ inch strips

8 green onions, with the green tops trimmed to 3 inches

8 (10 inch) flour tortillas, warmed

2 cups shredded romaine lettuce

Salsa

1 lb. ripe tomatoes, preferably plum tomatoes, peeled, seeded and minced

1 green bell pepper, diced

1 small onion, minced

1 to 3 jalapeño peppers, seeded and minced

2 tbsp. fresh lime juice

2 tbsp. chopped fresh cilantro

¼ tsp. salt

Mix the lime juice, tequila, chili powder, oregano, cumin and pepper in a shallow, nonreactive dish. Add the steak strips and toss them to coat. Refrigerate them for 30 minutes.

Make the salsa: Mix the tomatoes, bell pepper, onion, jalapeño pepper, lime juice, cilantro and salt together in a medium bowl. Let this stand for at least 15 minutes so the flavors can blend.

Preheat the broiler or get the grill ready. If broiling, line a broiler pan with foil.

Put the steak and the green onions on the foil-lined pan or grill. Cook them about 1 minute on each side or until the steak is medium-rare and the onions are lightly charred. Then, cut the steak strips into 1 inch pieces.

To serve, put some of the steak pieces and juices on each tortilla and top with some shredded lettuce, a scallion and then some salsa. Roll them up and serve at once, passing the remaining salsa with them.

4 Servings

"A*lso known as Southwestern succotash, this dish takes yellow squash and corn, and throws in some green chilies for emphasis. This one will keep the home fires burning.*"

MARIACHI VEGETABLES (CALABACITAS)

¼ cup butter

1 tbsp. olive oil

4 medium zucchini, halved lengthwise and cut into ½ inch slices

1 medium onion, chopped (about 1¼ cups)

1 medium red bell pepper, cut into thin strips

1 jalapeño pepper, seeded and minced

2 cloves garlic, minced

1 cup fresh corn kernels or frozen corn kernels, thawed and drained

½ cup heavy whipping cream

½ tsp. salt

¼ tsp. pepper

½ cup grated cheddar cheese (2 oz.)

In a large skillet, heat the butter and oil over medium-high heat until the butter is melted. Stir in the zucchini, onion, bell pepper, jalapeño pepper and garlic and cook about 5 minutes or until the zucchini is slightly softened.

Then, stir in the corn, cream, salt and pepper. Lower the heat, cover and simmer it about 5 minutes or until it is heated through.

Remove the skillet from the heat and stir in the cheese until it's melted. Serve at once.

4 Servings

"❝ ***T**ake the flaky, latticed crust of traditional American pie, fill it with tomatoes and jalapeños, and you have Tex-Mex pie. For an even flakier, much thicker crust, check out Vice President Stryker's skull.*"

TEX-MEX LATTICE-TOPPED PIE

Pastry

1¾ cups flour

¾ cup cornmeal

½ tsp. salt

6 tbsp. cold butter, cut into pieces

4 tbsp. cold shortening

1½ cups shredded cheddar cheese (6 oz.)

About 6 tbsp. ice water

Filling

1 tbsp. olive oil

1 large onion, chopped

4 cloves garlic, minced

1 lb. lean ground beef

2 medium pickled jalapeño peppers, seeded and minced

2 tbsp. chili powder

2 tsp. ground cumin

1½ tsp. oregano

4 large plum tomatoes, chopped

5 green onions, chopped

1 egg yolk

1 tbsp. milk

3 large romaine lettuce leaves, shredded

½ cup sour cream

Make the pastry: Mix the flour, cornmeal and salt together. Cut in the butter and shortening until the mixture looks like coarse meal. Then, stir in 1 cup of the cheddar cheese. Sprinkle this with 4 tbsp. of the ice water and lightly toss with a fork to form a dough, adding up to 2 tbsp. more ice water, if necessary.

Form ⅔ of the dough into a disc and the remaining ⅓ of the dough into another disc. Wrap each in plastic wrap and refrigerate them while you make the filling.

Make the filling: In a large skillet, cook and stir the onion and garlic in the olive oil over medium-high heat for 5 minutes. Add the beef and cook and stir it for 3 to 5 minutes or until it's no longer pink. Stir in the jalapeño peppers, chili powder, cumin and oregano and cook for 1 minute. Remove the skillet from the heat and stir in ⅓ cup each of the tomatoes and green onions.

Preheat the oven to 425°F.

Roll out the larger disc of dough on a floured surface into an 11 inch circle and fit it into a 9 inch pie pan. Roll out the other disc of dough into a 10 inch circle and cut it into 8 strips.

Spoon the filling into the pie shell and sprinkle it with the remaining ½ cup cheese. Put 4 strips of dough across the pie and put the remaining 4 strips of dough across the pie so that they're perpendicular to the first set of strips. Crimp the ends of the strips to seal them to the rim of the pie crust.

Mix the egg yolk and milk together and brush it over the top of the pie.

Bake it for 17 to 20 minutes or until it's golden brown.

Serve the pie with the remaining tomatoes, green onions, the shredded lettuce and the sour cream.

8 Servings

MEXICAN RICE

2 tbsp. vegetable oil

1 cup uncooked long-grain white rice

1 small onion, minced

1 large clove garlic, minced

1 small green bell pepper, cut into ¼ inch strips

1 medium tomato, diced

1 tsp. salt

1 tsp. chili powder

2 cups chicken broth

In a medium saucepan, heat the oil until it is almost smoking. Add the rice and cook and stir it until the rice is golden brown.

Stir in the onion, garlic and bell pepper and cook for 1 minute. Then, stir in the tomato, salt and chili powder and cook for 1 more minute.

Add the chicken broth and bring it to a boil. Lower the heat, cover and simmer it for 18 to 20 minutes or until the rice is tender and has absorbed all the liquid.

Serve the rice hot.

4 Servings

"**O**ne *4th of July I tried turning this Red, Green and Gold Casserole into a red, white and blue meal by substituting tomatoes, endive and blue cheese for the real ingredients. Take my advice—stick to the recipe here. It's every bit as American, and a whole lot tastier!*"

RED, GOLD AND GREEN SKILLET CASSEROLE

1 tbsp. olive or other vegetable oil

1 tbsp. butter

1 medium onion, coarsely chopped

2 cloves garlic, minced

4 medium plum tomatoes, coarsely chopped

1 medium green bell pepper, coarsely chopped

2 cups chicken broth

1 can (4 oz.) diced green chilies, drained (optional)

½ tsp. oregano

¼ tsp. pepper

½ lb. small tube pasta, such as ditalini (about 2¼ cups)

1½ cups grated Monterey Jack cheese

Preheat the broiler.

In a large ovenproof skillet, heat the oil and butter until the butter is melted. Stir in the onion and garlic and cook them about 5 minutes or until the onion begins to brown.

Stir in the tomatoes, bell pepper, chicken broth, chilies, if desired, oregano and pepper. Bring this to a boil and add the pasta. Then, lower the heat and simmer it about 9 minutes or until the pasta is just tender. Stir in 1 cup of the Monterey Jack cheese, then sprinkle with the remaining ½ cup cheese.

Broil the casserole 4 inches from the heat for 3 to 5 minutes or until it's golden brown.

6 Servings

POSOLE

2 lbs. pork shoulder

3½ cups beef broth

3 cups water

2 medium onions, 1 sliced and
   1 chopped

5 cloves garlic, 2 whole and 3 minced

¾ tsp. oregano

½ tsp. salt

2 tbsp. olive oil

2 tbsp. chili powder

2 cans (16 oz. each) hominy, drained

3 medium tomatoes, chopped (about
   3 cups) or 1 can (28 oz.) whole
   tomatoes, drained and chopped

1 can (4 oz.) diced green chilies,
   drained

1 cup chopped fresh cilantro (optional)

1 medium yellow or green bell
   pepper, cut into ½ inch pieces

4 cups shredded lettuce

10 radishes, sliced

2 limes, cut into wedges

1 avocado, diced and sprinkled with
   lime juice

Buttered hot corn tortillas

In a large saucepan, bring the pork, beef broth, water, the sliced onion, the
2 whole cloves of garlic, the oregano and the salt to a boil. Lower the heat,
cover and simmer it for 2 hours.

Remove the pork and strain the broth through a colander that has been lined
with 2 thicknesses of dampened cheesecloth. Either skim the fat from the
broth or refrigerate it until the fat hardens and remove it then. Set the broth
aside and cut the pork into ½ inch cubes.

In a Dutch oven or flameproof casserole, cook and stir the chopped onion and
the minced garlic in the olive oil until the onion is softened, but not browned.

Add the cubed pork and the chili powder and cook and stir them for
1 to 2 minutes.

Add the reserved pork broth, hominy,
tomatoes, green chilies and cilantro, if
desired. Cover and simmer this for 20
minutes, then stir in the bell pepper
and simmer 15 more minutes.

Serve the posole with the shredded
lettuce, radishes, lime wedges, avocado and buttered tortillas on the side.

8 Servings

"Sopaipillas, or puffed fried bread with cinnamon sugar, are to New Mexicans what danish are to New Yorkers. Only without the attitude."**

SOPAIPILLAS

¼ cup sugar

2 tsp. cinnamon

2 cups flour

2 tsp. baking powder

½ tsp. salt

2 tbsp. cold butter

⅔ cup water

Peanut oil for deep-frying

Mix the sugar and cinnamon together and set aside.

Mix the flour, baking powder and the salt together in a medium bowl. Cut in the butter until the mixture looks like coarse meal. Sprinkle this with the ice water and lightly toss with a fork until the dough is just moistened and it's still crumbly.

Turn the dough out onto a floured surface and knead it until it's smooth. Shape it into a ball and let it sit for 10 minutes.

In a Dutch oven or deep-fryer, heat 2 inches of oil to 375°F.

Roll out the dough into a ¼ inch thick rectangle. Then, cut the dough into 2½ inch squares.

Fry the dough squares in the hot oil, a few at a time, for 2 to 4 minutes or until they're puffed and golden brown, gently turning them with tongs.

Drain them on paper towels and, while they're still hot, dredge them in the sugar-cinnamon mixture.

About 3 Dozen Sopaipillas

FRESH FRUIT SALAD WITH MINT AND COCONUT

6 cups honeydew melon cubes (about 1 medium melon)

6 cups fresh pineapple slices, quartered (about 1 medium pineapple)

3 cups kiwi fruit slices (about 8 kiwi fruit)

3 cups papaya cubes (about 1 medium papaya)

1½ cups mango cubes (about 2 mangoes)

1 cup grated fresh coconut or unsweetened shredded coconut

¾ cup lime juice

¾ cup frozen orange juice concentrate, thawed

6 tbsp. honey

¾ cup chopped fresh mint

In a large serving bowl, combine the honeydew, pineapple, kiwi fruit, papaya, mango and ¾ cup of the coconut.

Mix the lime juice, orange juice concentrate and honey together and pour over the fruit; toss it to combine. Then, cover and refrigerate it for at least 1 hour.

To serve, sprinkle the salad with the mint and the remaining ¼ cup coconut.

About 18 Servings

Turkey Cutlets with Apricots and Cream, page 103

THE WEST COAST

Avocado and Grapefruit Salad with Poppy-Seed Dressing

Caesar Salad with Grilled Chicken Breasts

Cobb Salad

Oriental Grilled Fish Salad

Grilled Beef Tenderloin Steaks with Roasted Garlic Sauce

Shallow-Fried Fish Tempura with Two Sauces

Skillet-Baked Trout with Lemon-Caper Sauce

Hangtown Fry

Chicken Thighs Teriyaki

Tuna Burgers

Vegetable Lo Mein

Turkey Cutlets with Apricots and Cream

Baked Radiatore with Salmon and White Cheddar Sauce

Roasted Salmon with Carrots, Mushrooms and New Potatoes

Sourdough Bread

Pound Cake with Pears and Raspberry Sauce

Carlo's Chocolate Earthquake Cake

Homemade Granola

"**Y**ou'll be surprised how well the acidic juice of the grapefruit cuts the natural fat of the avocado in this salad. It reminds me of the way Hillary interacts with Bill!"

AVOCADO AND GRAPEFRUIT SALAD WITH POPPY-SEED DRESSING

Dressing

2 tbsp. distilled white vinegar

2 tbsp. sugar

¼ tsp. dry mustard

⅛ tsp. salt

3½ tbsp. light olive oil

1 tbsp. poppy seed

Salad

24 cherry tomatoes, halved

4 small Belgian endive, each cut
   into 2 inch lengths

2 pink grapefruit, peeled and sectioned

2 small avocados, peeled and cubed

1 cup chopped green onions (about 5 medium)

Make the dressing: Whisk the vinegar, sugar, dry mustard and salt together in a small bowl until the sugar and salt are dissolved. While whisking constantly, add the oil in a slow stream until the dressing is thick and smooth. Stir in the poppy seed.

Make the salad: Combine the tomatoes, endive, grapefruit, avocado and green onions in a large bowl. Pour the dressing over the salad and toss it gently.

6 Servings

CAESAR SALAD WITH GRILLED CHICKEN BREASTS

4 oz. Italian or French bread, cut into ½ inch slices

2 cloves garlic, peeled and halved

3 tbsp. fresh lemon juice

½ tsp. salt

½ tsp. oregano

¼ tsp. freshly ground pepper

1 lb. skinless boneless chicken breasts

½ cup reduced-sodium chicken broth, fat removed

3 tbsp. reduced-fat mayonnaise

1 tbsp. reduced-fat sour cream

1 tsp. anchovy paste

5 cups torn romaine lettuce

8 cherry tomatoes, halved

1 tbsp. capers, rinsed and drained

Preheat the oven to 400°F.

Put the bread on a baking sheet and bake it for 5 minutes or until it's crisp and golden brown. Immediately rub the bread with the cut sides of the garlic. Then, cut the bread into cubes for croutons and set them aside.

Preheat the broiler or get the grill ready. If broiling, line a broiler pan with foil.

Mix 1 tbsp. of the lemon juice, salt, oregano and pepper. Rub this mixture over the chicken.

Broil the chicken on the foil-lined broiler pan or grill 6 inches from the heat for about 5 minutes on each side or until the chicken is tender and the juices run clear. When cool enough to handle, cut the chicken into strips.

Whisk the broth, mayonnaise, sour cream, anchovy paste and the remaining 2 tbsp. lemon juice together in a large bowl. Add the lettuce, tomatoes, capers and the croutons and toss it to coat with the broth mixture.

Put the salad in 4 bowls, then top it with the sliced chicken and serve.

4 Servings

"**R**ita, the White House cook, hid me and Matt Douglas under several hundred heads of lettuce. The whole time, I was planning the delicious Cobb Salad I'd make if I ever got out of this mess."

COBB SALAD

Dressing

⅔ cup plain nonfat yogurt

3 tbsp. ketchup

1 tbsp. fresh lemon juice

½ tsp. salt

¼ tsp. freshly ground pepper

Salad

6 cups chopped romaine lettuce

2 red bell peppers, diced and blanched

2 cups frozen peas, thawed

8 green onions, thinly sliced

3 oz. crumbled blue cheese or feta cheese

2 hard-cooked egg whites, coarsely chopped

Make the dressing: Whisk together the yogurt, ketchup, lemon juice, salt and pepper until well blended and set it aside.

Make the salad: Cover a serving platter with the lettuce. Put the bell peppers in a row down the center of the lettuce, then put 1 cup of the peas in a row next to the bell peppers on each side. Put the green onions next to the peas on one side, then half of the cheese next to the green onions. On the other side of the peas, put the egg whites, then the rest of the cheese.

Serve the salad with the dressing.

4 Servings

ORIENTAL GRILLED FISH SALAD

4 quarter-size slices (¼ inch thick) fresh ginger, unpeeled

2 cloves garlic

¼ cup reduced-sodium soy sauce

3 tbsp. lime juice

2 tbsp. vegetable oil

1 tbsp. honey

1 tsp. grated lime rind (optional)

¼ tsp. pepper

¼ tsp. red pepper flakes

1¼ lbs. cod or halibut steaks

4 cups shredded Napa or Chinese cabbage (about 6 oz.)

4 cups shredded red leaf lettuce (about ½ head)

2 large carrots, cut into thin strips

2 cups bean sprouts (about ¼ lb.)

2 tbsp. sesame seed, toasted (optional)

Preheat the broiler or get the grill ready. If broiling, line a broiler pan with foil.

Mince the ginger and garlic in a food processor. Add the soy sauce, lime juice, oil, honey, lime rind, if desired, pepper and red pepper flakes and process this until it's blended. Set aside half of this mixture for the salad dressing.

Put the fish on the foil-lined broiler pan or grill and baste it with the other half of the ginger mixture. Broil or grill the fish 4 inches from the heat for about 5 minutes on each side or until the fish flakes easily with a fork, turning it once and basting again with the ginger mixture.

Meanwhile, divide the cabbage, lettuce, carrots and bean sprouts evenly among 4 dinner plates.

Cut the hot fish into ¾ inch pieces and put them on top of the vegetables. Then, pour the dressing on top and sprinkle with the sesame seed.

4 Servings

TIP: To toast sesame seeds, put them in a small microwave-safe bowl and toss them with 1 tsp. of oil. Cook at 100% for 4 to 6 minutes or just until they begin to brown (they will continue to brown after cooking), stirring them once or twice.

"This recipe calls for two whole bulbs of garlic, which is a lot of garlic power. Use it wisely. I often ate this just before a long filibuster, and I found that two healthy servings will produce enough, shall we say, aroma to empty the Senate."

GRILLED BEEF TENDERLOIN STEAKS WITH ROASTED GARLIC SAUCE

2 whole garlic bulbs, cloves separated, but not peeled

1 tsp. cracked black peppercorns

½ tsp. juniper berries, crushed

4 beef tenderloin steaks (about ¼ lb. each)

1 cup dry red wine

3 shallots, sliced or ½ small onion, minced

2 cups beef broth or chicken broth

Preheat the oven to 500°F.

Put the garlic cloves in a small baking dish and bake them for 20 to 30 minutes or until they're soft. Let them cool.

Preheat the broiler or get the grill ready. If broiling, line a broiler pan with foil.

Mix the peppercorns and juniper berries together. Press this mixture onto the steaks and set them aside.

In a small nonreactive saucepan, boil the wine and the shallots over medium-high heat about 5 minutes or until nearly all the wine has evaporated. Then, add the beef broth. Boil this mixture about 5 minutes more or until it is reduced to about 1 cup.

Squeeze the garlic pulp from the skins into a food processor or a blender. Pour in the broth mixture and process this until it's thick and smooth. Then return it to the saucepan and keep it warm.

Broil or grill the steaks 4 inches from the heat for about 3 minutes on each side for medium-rare.

Serve the steaks with the garlic sauce.

4 Servings

SHALLOW-FRIED FISH TEMPURA WITH TWO SAUCES

Ginger-Soy Sauce

2 quarter-size slices (¼ inch thick)
    fresh ginger, unpeeled and minced

3 tbsp. reduced-sodium or regular soy
    sauce

2 tbsp. cider vinegar

1½ tsp. sesame oil

½ tsp. pepper

⅛ tsp. red pepper flakes

Tartar Sauce

¼ cup mayonnaise

¼ cup plain yogurt

3 tbsp. pickle relish, drained

Fish Tempura

⅓ cup cornstarch

2 tbsp. flour

½ tsp. salt

½ tsp. baking powder

1 egg lightly beaten with 2 tbsp. water

1 cup vegetable oil

1 lb. firm-fleshed white fish fillets, like
    scrod, cut into 1½ inch pieces

Make the ginger-soy sauce: Mix the ginger, soy sauce, vinegar, sesame oil, ⅛ tsp. of the pepper and the red pepper flakes together and set it aside.

Make the tartar sauce: Mix the mayonnaise, yogurt, ⅛ tsp. of the pepper and pickle relish together and refrigerate it.

Make the fish tempura: Mix the cornstarch, flour, salt, baking powder and remaining ¼ tsp. pepper together in a medium bowl. Stir the egg-water mixture into the dry ingredients and blend it well.

In a small heavy saucepan, heat the oil until it's hot, but not smoking (375°F). Cook the fish in small batches about 3 minutes or until they're golden brown and flake easily with a fork, turning them once or twice. Drain the fish on paper towels.

Serve the fish with the sauces on the side.

4 Servings

"The Democrats probably could've used some of this caper-based sauce before breaking into the Watergate complex. Guess they were about as smart as the brook trout I caught at Camp David."

SKILLET-BAKED TROUT WITH LEMON-CAPER SAUCE

3 slices bacon	2 tbsp. olive or other vegetable oil
½ cup flour	3 tbsp. lemon juice
½ cup cornmeal	2 tbsp. butter
½ tsp. pepper	2 tbsp. capers, rinsed and drained
¼ tsp. salt	2 tsp. grated lemon rind
4 small whole brook trout (about ½ lb. each)	¼ cup chopped parsley (optional)

Preheat the oven to 425°F.

In a large ovenproof skillet, cook the bacon until it's crisp. Remove the bacon and reserve 1 tbsp. of the drippings in the skillet.

Mix the flour, cornmeal, pepper and salt together in a shallow bowl. Then, dredge the fish in the flour mixture, shaking off any excess.

Add 1 tbsp. of the olive oil to the reserved bacon drippings and heat it until it's hot but not smoking (375°F). Then, add the fish and cook them about 2 minutes on each side or until they're brown, adding the remaining 1 tbsp. oil, if necessary, to keep them from sticking.

Put the fish in the skillet in the oven and bake it for 15 minutes or until the fish flake easily with a fork. Put one fish on each of 4 individual dinner plates and keep them warm.

Return the skillet to the stovetop. Add the lemon juice, butter, capers, lemon rind and parsley, if desired. Cook and stir this for about 1 minute or until the butter is melted and the mixture is heated through.

Crumble the bacon. Then, pour the lemon-caper sauce over the fish and sprinkle with the crumbled bacon.

4 Servings

HANGTOWN FRY

¼ lb. bacon (4 to 6 slices)

12 unsalted saltine crackers, finely crushed

¼ cup flour

⅜ tsp. pepper

½ tsp. salt

6 eggs

2 tbsp. milk

½ pt. shucked oysters, drained and patted dry

2 tbsp. butter

2 tbsp. chopped fresh parsley

1 tbsp. chopped fresh chives (optional)

1 lemon, cut into wedges

In a large skillet, cook the bacon until it's crisp. Remove the bacon and reserve the drippings in the skillet.

Mix the crushed crackers, flour, ¼ tsp. of the pepper and ¼ tsp. of the salt in a shallow bowl. Beat 1 of the eggs with the milk in another bowl. Then, dip the oysters first in the egg mixture, then dredge in the cracker mixture. Reserve the remaining egg mixture.

In the same skillet, melt the butter in the bacon drippings over medium heat. Then, add the oysters and cook them for 2 to 4 minutes or until they're golden brown.

Meanwhile, beat the remaining 5 eggs with the reserved egg mixture, the parsley, the chives, if desired, and the remaining ⅛ tsp. pepper and ¼ tsp. salt.

Pour this mixture over the oysters in the skillet. Then, cook the eggs for 3 to 4 minutes or until they're set, lifting them with a spatula to let the uncooked eggs flow underneath.

Crumble the bacon. Sprinkle the oysters with the crumbled bacon and serve them with the lemon wedges.

4 Servings

" **I**'ve been famous for preparing this recipe with boneless breasts since I was a junior Congressman. But as I've matured into the golden years of my manhood, I've become a thigh man."

CHICKEN THIGHS TERIYAKI

Marinade

2 quarter-size slices (¼ inch thick) fresh ginger, peeled and chopped

1 large clove garlic, minced

⅔ cup sake

½ cup Japanese soy sauce

2 tbsp. sugar

Chicken

8 chicken thighs, skin removed

2 tsp. cornstarch

Make the marinade: Put the ginger, garlic, sake, soy sauce and sugar in a food processor or blender. Process about 1 minute or until the mixture is fairly smooth. Strain the marinade into a shallow dish.

Score the chicken thighs in a diamond pattern, ¼ inch deep and ½ inch apart. Put the chicken, scored-side-down, in the marinade. Put it in the refrigerator for 30 minutes, turning the chicken twice.

Meanwhile, preheat the broiler. Line a broiler pan with foil.

Remove the chicken from the marinade. Reserve 1 cup of the marinade and put it in a small saucepan.

Put the chicken thighs, scored-side-down, on the foil-lined broiler pan. Broil them 5 inches from the heat for 12 to 14 minutes or until they're browned and the juices run clear, turning them once. Put 2 chicken thighs on each of 4 dinner plates.

Mix the reserved marinade and the cornstarch together. Bring this to a boil and cook and stir it for 1 to 2 minutes or until it's thickened.

Coat each chicken thigh with about 1 tbsp. of the teriyaki glaze and serve the rest of it in a sauceboat.

4 Servings

TUNA BURGERS

1 small red onion, quartered

1 stalk celery, quartered

2 cans (6½ oz. each) water-pack
   solid white tuna, well drained

1 egg

3 slices whole wheat or white bread,
   torn into large pieces

2 tbsp. butter

2 tsp. Dijon mustard

¼ tsp. cayenne pepper

¼ tsp. pepper

About ¼ cup flour

2 tbsp. olive or other vegetable oil

Put the onion and celery in a food processor and pulse it until they're coarsely chopped.

Add the tuna and process it briefly just to break it up.

Add the egg, bread, butter, Dijon mustard, cayenne pepper and the pepper and process it just until it's blended.

Put the flour in a shallow bowl. Lightly flour your hands and shape the tuna mixture into 4 patties about 4 inches in diameter. Dredge the patties lightly in the flour.

In a large nonstick skillet, heat the oil until it's hot, but not smoking (375°F). Cook the patties about 3 minutes on each side or until they're browned.

Serve them hot.

4 Servings

"**D**uring the halcyon days when I was in residence at the White House, I used to send out for Chinese food quite a bit. The problem was that by the time the bomb squad got finished checking my order, it was cold and had been thoroughly sniffed by German shepherds. Now I cook my own."

VEGETABLE LO MEIN

⅔ cup chicken broth

¼ cup reduced-sodium soy sauce

1 tsp. cornstarch

1 tsp. dry sherry (optional)

3 drops hot pepper sauce

¼ tsp. red pepper flakes

¼ tsp. pepper

¾ lb. uncooked linguine or spaghetti

2 tbsp. vegetable oil

5 quarter-size slices (¼ inch thick) fresh ginger, unpeeled and minced

3 cloves garlic, minced

4 green onions, chopped

1 large red bell pepper, coarsely chopped

½ head small cabbage, shredded

¼ lb. small mushrooms

¼ lb. fresh spinach, torn into smaller pieces

¼ lb. fresh bean sprouts

¼ cup (packed) cilantro sprigs, minced (optional)

Mix the chicken broth, soy sauce, cornstarch, sherry, if desired, hot pepper sauce, red pepper flakes and pepper together and set it aside.

Cook the linguine according to the package directions; drain and set it aside.

While the linguine is cooking, in a large skillet or wok, heat 1 tbsp. of the oil until it's hot, but not smoking (375°F). Add the ginger and the garlic and cook and stir them about 2 minutes or until they're fragrant.

Add the remaining 1 tbsp. oil, then the green onions, bell pepper, cabbage, mushrooms, spinach and bean sprouts. Cook and stir them about 4 minutes or until the vegetables begin to soften.

Add the linguine and the chicken broth mixture to the skillet. Bring this to a boil while tossing the ingredients together. Add the cilantro, if desired, and cook about 2 minutes more or until it is heated through.

4 Servings

TURKEY CUTLETS WITH APRICOTS AND CREAM

3 tbsp. flour

¾ tsp. salt

¼ tsp. pepper

8 small turkey cutlets (about 1¼ lbs. total)

2 tbsp. butter

2 tbsp. vegetable oil

4 quarter-size slices (¼ inch thick) fresh ginger, unpeeled and minced

5 medium shallots, minced (about ¼ lb.) or 1 medium onion, minced

¾ cup dried apricots, diced (about 5 oz.)

¾ cup chicken broth

¼ cup sweet vermouth or chicken broth

1 tsp. basil

½ tsp. sugar

½ cup heavy whipping cream

Preheat the oven to its lowest temperature.

Mix the flour, salt and pepper together in a shallow bowl. Then, dredge the turkey in the flour mixture, shaking off any excess. Reserve the rest of the flour mixture.

In a large skillet, heat 1 tbsp. of the butter and 1 tbsp. of the oil over medium-high heat until the butter is melted. Add 4 of the turkey cutlets and cook them about 3 minutes on each side or until they're browned. Put the turkey on a heatproof platter and keep it warm in the oven while you cook the rest of the turkey in the remaining 1 tbsp. butter and 1 tbsp. oil.

Then, add the ginger and shallots to the skillet and cook and stir them about 1 minute or until the shallots are slightly softened. Stir in the reserved flour mixture and cook and stir it for 30 seconds.

Add the apricots, chicken broth, vermouth, basil and sugar and bring this to a boil. Lower the heat, cover and simmer for 5 minutes.

Then, bring this mixture back to a boil and stir in the cream and any juices that have accumulated on the plate under the turkey.

Serve the turkey topped with the sauce.

4 Servings

"**F**or those who think radiatore is a dish of radiator parts from an Italian car, this recipe of mine should bring you up to speed in a hurry!"

BAKED RADIATORE WITH SALMON AND WHITE CHEDDAR SAUCE

¾ lb. uncooked radiatore pasta (about 1½ cups)

¼ cup butter

2 cloves garlic, minced

⅓ cup flour

1¼ cups milk

1 cup grated white cheddar cheese (4 oz.)

1½ tsp. dill weed

½ tsp. salt

¼ tsp. white pepper

1 medium red bell pepper, diced

1 medium green bell pepper, diced

1 can (7½ oz.) salmon, drained

3 tbsp. grated Parmesan cheese

Preheat the oven to 425°F. Butter a 13 inch x 9 inch baking dish.

In a large saucepan, cook the radiatore according to the package directions; drain and return it to the saucepan.

Meanwhile, melt the butter in a medium saucepan Add the garlic and cook and stir it for 1 minute. Stir in the flour and cook it for 30 seconds. Then, slowly stir in the milk and cook until it's smooth, stirring constantly.

Stir in the cheddar cheese, dill weed, salt and pepper and cook until the cheese is melted, stirring constantly.

Gently stir the cheese sauce into the radiatore, along with the red bell pepper, the green bell pepper and the salmon.

Put this mixture into the baking dish and sprinkle it with the Parmesan cheese. Bake it for 15 minutes or until it's heated through and just beginning to brown.

6 Servings

"*O*ur guide on a recent fly-fishing trip to Oregon taught me this superb recipe for salmon. I love the whole zen-like experience of waiting patiently for a wily fish to take my lure. On this particular trip, however, if I remember correctly, we used canned salmon."

ROASTED SALMON WITH CARROTS, MUSHROOMS AND NEW POTATOES

¼ cup olive or other vegetable oil

¼ cup chopped parsley (optional)

2 cloves garlic, minced

¾ tsp. salt

¼ tsp. pepper

8 small red potatoes, unpeeled and quartered (about 1 lb.)

2 large carrots, cut diagonally into ½ inch slices

3 green onions, cut into 2 inch pieces

½ lb. whole small mushrooms or large mushrooms, halved

1 lb. salmon fillets, cut into 1½ inch cubes

Preheat the oven to 450°F.

Stir the oil, parsley, if desired, garlic, salt and pepper together in a medium bowl.

Scatter the potatoes, carrots, green onions and mushrooms over the bottom of a shallow 1½-quart baking dish. Drizzle them with 2 tbsp. of the oil mixture and toss them to coat. Add the salmon to the remaining oil mixture and toss gently to coat.

Bake the vegetables about 30 minutes or until the potatoes are almost done and beginning to brown, stirring them once or twice.

Lower the oven temperature to 375°F. Gently stir the vegetables, scatter the salmon on top and bake about 10 more minutes or until the vegetables are tender and the salmon flakes easily with a fork.

4 Servings

SOURDOUGH BREAD

Sourdough Starter

2½ cups flour

2½ cups lukewarm water (105°F to 115°F)

2 tsp. sugar

1 package active dry yeast

Bread

2 cups sourdough starter

1 package active dry yeast

¼ cup lukewarm water (105°F to 115°F)

2 tsp. salt

2 tsp. sugar

4½ to 5 cups flour

2 tbsp. butter, softened

2 tsp. cornmeal

Make the starter: At least 3 days before you plan to make the bread, mix the flour, lukewarm water, sugar and yeast together in a large glass jar. Cover the jar loosely and let it stand 3 to 5 days in a warm, draft-free place, stirring once a day with a wooden spoon. It should have a pleasant sour smell and should be thick and filled with small bubbles. If it isn't, the yeast isn't working and you should start over with fresh yeast. If you don't want to use the starter right away, cover it tightly and refrigerate it.

Make the bread: If the starter has been refrigerated, take out 2 cups of it, put it in a large bowl and let it stand at room temperature for 2 hours.

Dissolve the yeast in the lukewarm water. Stir the yeast mixture, the salt and the sugar into the starter. Add 4½ cups of the flour and stir it until the mixture forms a dough, adding up to ½ cup more flour, if necessary. Then beat in the butter.

On a lightly floured surface, knead the dough about 10 minutes or until it's smooth and elastic. Shape the dough into a ball and put it in a large greased bowl. Cover the bowl with a slightly damp kitchen towel and let the dough rise in a warm, draft-free place until it doubles in size, about 1½ hours.

Lightly sprinkle a large baking sheet with the cornmeal. Punch the dough down, then knead it on a lightly floured surface for 1 to 2 minutes.

Divide the dough in half. Shape each half into an 8 inch x 4 inch loaf. Put the loaves on the baking sheet and sprinkle them lightly with flour. Then, using a kitchen scissors, make a zigzag line of deep cuts lengthwise along the top of each loaf.

Brush the tops of the loaves with a little water and let them rise again in a warm, draft-free place until they're double in size, 35 to 45 minutes.

Meanwhile, preheat the oven to 375°F. Bake the loaves for 30 minutes or until they're well browned and they sound hollow when thumped on the bottom.

Two 8 inch Loaves

> "**I** got this delicious dessert recipe in beautiful sunny California, my favorite state. The best people, the most marvelous wines, the most spectacular weather, the most electoral votes."

POUND CAKE WITH PEARS AND RASPBERRY SAUCE

1 package (10 oz.) frozen raspberries in light syrup

2 tbsp. cornstarch

8 slices pound cake, ½ inch thick

2 small pears, unpeeled, cored and cut into ¼ inch thick wedges

Break the frozen raspberries into 3 or 4 chunks and put them in a food processor. Process them until they're smooth.

Mix the raspberries and the cornstarch together in a small saucepan. Bring this to a boil and cook for 1 to 2 minutes or until it's thickened. Remove it from the heat and set it aside to cool.

Put 2 slices of pound cake on each of 4 dessert plates. Then top the cake slices with the pear wedges and some of the raspberry sauce.

4 Servings

"If you want to live really dangerously, cut yourself a big slab of this chocolate cake. I guarantee the earth will move for you, too."

CARLO'S CHOCOLATE EARTHQUAKE CAKE

2 cups powdered sugar

¼ cup potato flour or all-purpose flour

12 oz. semi-sweet chocolate

½ cup unsalted butter

4 eggs, at room temperature

2 tbsp. grated orange rind

1 tsp. vanilla

Preheat the oven to 350°F. Generously butter and flour an 8 inch round cake pan and line the bottom with a circle of wax paper. Butter the wax paper.

Sift the powdered sugar and flour together and set them aside.

In the top of a double boiler, over hot, not simmering, water, melt the chocolate and the butter. Stir this until it's smooth. Put it in a bowl and let it cool slightly.

Wash the upper part of the double boiler and put the eggs in it. Put it over simmering water and, using an electric mixer at high speed, beat them for 10 to 15 minutes or until they've doubled in volume and are light-colored, creamy and form soft peaks.

Gently, with a wooden spoon, stir the chocolate mixture into the eggs. Stir the sugar and the flour mixture, a third at a time, into the chocolate-egg mixture. Stir in the orange rind and vanilla.

Then, pour the batter into the pan and bake it for 30 minutes. Cool the cake before removing it from the pan.

One 8 inch Cake

HOMEMADE GRANOLA

1 cup rolled oats

½ cup wheat bran

½ cup whole blanched almonds

¼ cup untoasted
   sunflower nuts

2 tbsp. sesame seed

2 tsp. safflower oil

¼ tsp. salt

1 cup raisins

10 pitted dates, chopped

2 tbsp. honey

1 tsp. vanilla

Grated rind of 1 orange

Milk (optional)

Preheat the oven to 400°F.

Mix the oats, wheat bran, almonds, sunflower nuts, sesame seed, oil and salt together in a large bowl. Spread this mixture evenly in a 15½ inch x 10½ inch x 1 inch jelly-roll pan.

Bake it about 15 minutes or until it is lightly browned, stirring every 5 minutes.

Return this mixture to the bowl and stir in the raisins, dates, honey, vanilla and grated orange rind. Cool the granola completely and store it in an airtight container.

Serve the granola in individual bowls with milk, if desired.

8 Servings